LAWYER'S OMNIBUS

By Alex Steuart Williams

Law Brief Publishing

First published in 2013 by
Law Brief Publishing Ltd
Communications House
26 York Street
London
W1U 6PZ
www.lawbriefpublishing.com

Paperback: ISBN 978-0-9575530-1-9

Contents

FOREWORD

Most people would think that there's not a lot that's funny about either law or the people who practise it. First there's the reams of small print they have created along with the reputation for constant nit-picking. Then there are the huge bills, the funny clothes and the airs and graces that can creep up on the odd member of the profession as the years go by. But it's exactly these things which Alex Williams has so wonderfully turned to his comedic advantage. In gently teasing a profession he so evidently still cares about he has created a timeless classic of a cartoon strip that in my view will be still being read and chuckled along with a hundred years from now.

But his cartoons can appeal to more than lawyers since they reflect the weaknesses that make up so much of human nature such as vanity, greed, pettiness and ambition. They also reflect the contrast between what might be perceived as a high status profession and the reality of the daily grind which in fact takes up the lives of so many lawyers. Which of course might reflect on Alex's decision to leave a promising career at the Bar to follow the bright lights to Hollywood and beyond!

These cartoons are irreverent, funny, intelligent, mischievous and above all hugely likeable. All of which would also very accurately describe Alex himself. It is incredible to think that it is now twenty years since the first cartoon appeared in *The Times* and it is truly a privilege to be given this opportunity to publish this anniversary 'Best of' bumper edition.

Tim Kevan
Co-founder of Law Brief Publishing
Author of the BabyBarista blog and books
June 2013
Braunton, North Devon

INTRODUCTION

Queen's Counsel will be 20 years old this year. Which makes it the longest job I have ever managed to hold down by a very long way. The cartoon strip was started in 1993 by myself and my friend (and fellow law student) Graham Francis Defries. We cooked up the idea on a rainy day in the law library at Lincoln's Inn. A cartoon satire on lawyers seemed just the thing – it was the era of lawyer jokes and the OJ Simpson trial, a time when lawyers were even less popular than bankers.

After a brief flirtation with Private Eye and The Spectator we were lucky enough to get the strip published in The Times. And there it remains since, for reasons which remain unclear to this day, Rupert Murdoch has never quite gotten around to firing us.

Cast your mind back to the pre-internet age and you may recall that the law pages of The Times were required reading for all lawyers - the place to go for jobs, gossip, vacancies, news and law reports. In short – everything about law. At your law interview for some posh chambers or firm of solicitors, when a distinguished silk or partner asked you the inevitable question "what newspaper do you read?", there was only one sensible answer – "The Times". At the end of the 20th century some spoilsport invented the internet, and for newspapers it's been downhill ever since. The Times law pages have shrunk of late to just two skinny pages buried in the Thursday edition of the business section.

Still, Queen's Counsel is hanging in there, just like the beleaguered newspapers themselves, fighting off declining circulation and the threat of government regulation. And, just like The Times, Queen's Counsel is now online; you can see our shiny new website at www.qccartoon.com.

This book is the authoritative compendium – the very best of all the cartoon strips going back over twenty years. Two decades of making fun of lawyers – what more could anyone ask?

Alex Steuart Williams
London
2013

THE CHARACTERS

4 Lawn Buildings

1 2 3 4 5

1. Derek Hardman
Head clerk at 4 Lawn Buildings – and the power behind the throne. Publicly defers to the barristers in his chambers, but behind the scenes he deftly controls their careers.

2. Helena Fairchild
Junior barrister and human rights lawyer. Went into law to make a better world, but found to her disappointment that villains pay better than the angels. Wrestles with her conscience - and tries to do the right thing.

3. Quentin Crawley
Pupil barrister and all-round dogsbody. Desperate to win a tenancy. Hopeless in court – and lives in permanent terror that someone in chambers will notice.

4. Edward Longwind
Junior barrister and understudy to Sir Geoffrey, to whose levels of prosperity and pomposity Edward can only aspire. Thoroughly cynical and jaded. Desperate to take silk and add those magic letters "QC" to his name.

5. Sir Geoffrey Bentwood QC
Senior barrister, silk, part-time judge and Master of the Universe. Even his children call him "your honour". Longs to be promoted to the High Court so he can retire in comfort, splendour and ermine.

Fillibuster & Loophole

6   7   8

6. Richard Loophole
Senior partner at Fillibuster & Loophole. Legal fat cat, chief beneficiary of the fountain of cash that rises to the top of big law firms. Long ago forgot anything he learned at law school; delegates all the hard bits to his associates. Plays a lot of golf.

7. Rachel Underwood
Extremely bright and able associate solicitor; permanently on the verge of quitting her oppressive job. Works absurdly long hours. She is (in theory) entitled to holiday but can rarely take it. The firm promises to make her partner "some day". Her friends say she has Stockholm Syndrome.

8. Arthur Greybinder
Tax partner. Reads HM Revenue reports for fun. Motto: "the Code is Lord". A workaholic who is only vaguely aware of a family he has at home.

Judges & Clients

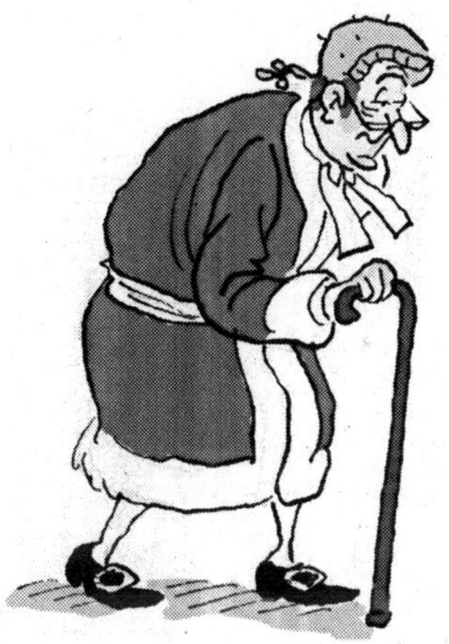

9

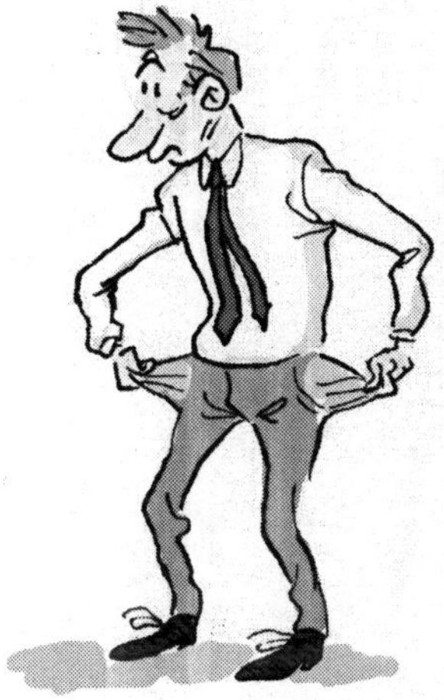

10

9. His Honour Judge Humphrey Barnacle
Formerly Head of Chambers at 4 Lawn Buildings, now put out to pasture in the courts. Hopelessly out of touch, and far more interested in gardening than the finer points of law and evidence.

10. Nigel Sprocket
The endlessly unlucky litigant whose lawyers will not rest until they have spent all of his money.

CHAPTER ONE
LAW SCHOOL

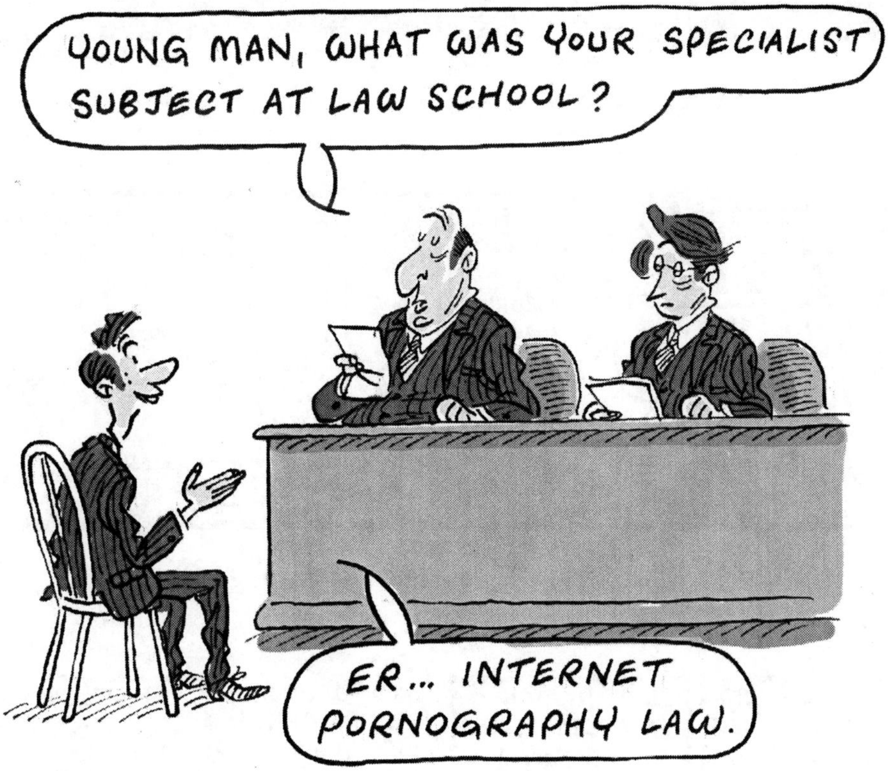
YOUNG MAN, WHAT WAS YOUR SPECIALIST SUBJECT AT LAW SCHOOL?
ER... INTERNET PORNOGRAPHY LAW.

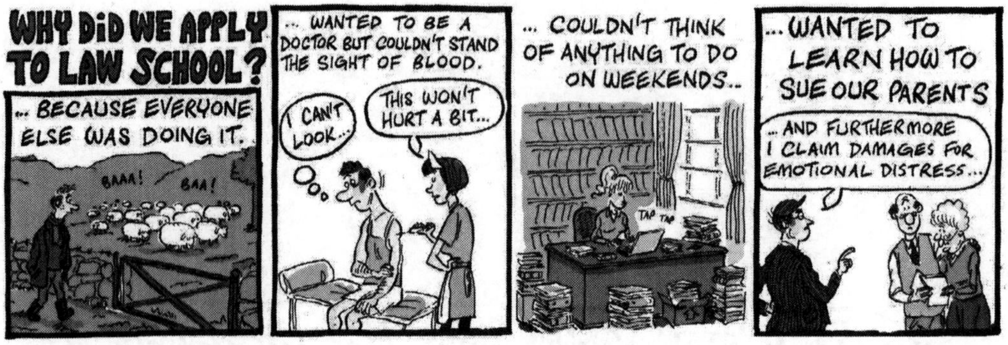
WHY DID WE APPLY TO LAW SCHOOL?
... BECAUSE EVERYONE ELSE WAS DOING IT.
BAAA!
BAA!
... WANTED TO BE A DOCTOR BUT COULDN'T STAND THE SIGHT OF BLOOD.
I CAN'T LOOK...
THIS WON'T HURT A BIT...
... COULDN'T THINK OF ANYTHING TO DO ON WEEKENDS...
TAP TAP
...WANTED TO LEARN HOW TO SUE OUR PARENTS
... AND FURTHERMORE I CLAIM DAMAGES FOR EMOTIONAL DISTRESS...

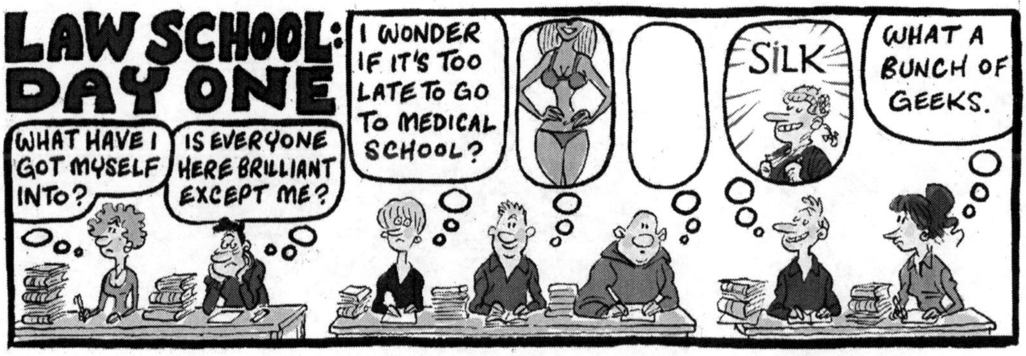
LAW SCHOOL: DAY ONE
WHAT HAVE I GOT MYSELF INTO?
IS EVERYONE HERE BRILLIANT EXCEPT ME?
I WONDER IF IT'S TOO LATE TO GO TO MEDICAL SCHOOL?
SILK
WHAT A BUNCH OF GEEKS.

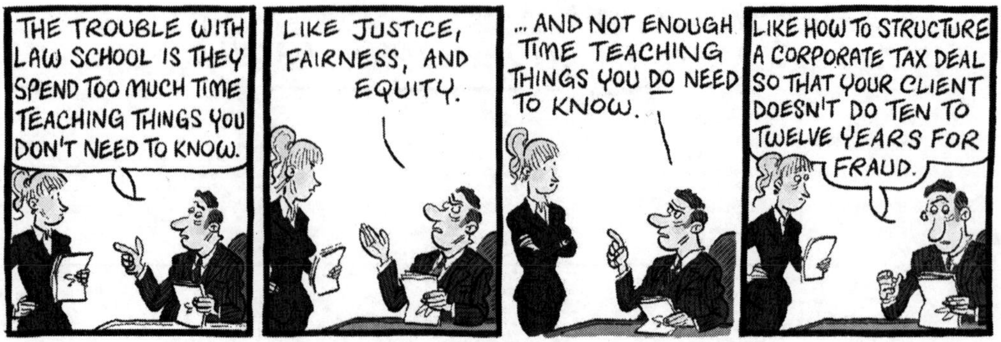
THE TROUBLE WITH LAW SCHOOL IS THEY SPEND TOO MUCH TIME TEACHING THINGS YOU DON'T NEED TO KNOW.
LIKE JUSTICE, FAIRNESS, AND EQUITY.
... AND NOT ENOUGH TIME TEACHING THINGS YOU DO NEED TO KNOW.
LIKE HOW TO STRUCTURE A CORPORATE TAX DEAL SO THAT YOUR CLIENT DOESN'T DO TEN TO TWELVE YEARS FOR FRAUD.

LAW SCHOOL HAZARDS
① VITAL PAGE RIPPED FROM TEXT BOOK THE WEEK BEFORE FINALS
② EVIL LECTURERS
YOU WILL ALL FAIL THE EXAM.
YOU'D BETTER BUY MY BOOK...
③ YOUR FAMILY
LAW? I HATE LAWYERS
WHY DON'T YOU DO SOMETHING USEFUL INSTEAD?
BET YOU WON'T PASS
④ OTHER STUDENTS.
I'VE GOT 7 INTERVIEWS THIS WEEK!
HAVEN'T YOU DONE THE HOMEWORK YET?
WHAT IF YOU FAIL?

LAW SCHOOL: - WHICH IS YOUR FAVOURITE SUBJECT?
REAL PROPERTY: LEARN HOW ANGLO-NORMAN FEUDAL TENURE STILL HAS RELEVANCE TODAY.
ENVIRONMENTAL LAW: HELP GIANT CORPORATIONS TO POLLUTE THE WATER-WAYS (AND GET AWAY WITH IT).
EVIDENCE: LEARN THE HEAR-SAY RULE AND ALL FIVE THOUSAND EXCEPTIONS.
Z Z
CRIMINAL LAW: STUDY WAYS TO DEFEND YOURSELF WHEN YOUR FRIENDS ASK YOU HOW YOU CAN ACT FOR RAPISTS AND MURDERERS.
INTERNET LAW: ASPIRE TO BE COUNSEL TO THE PORNOGRAPHY INDUSTRY.
!
CLICK

LAW STUDENT METAMORPHOSIS
1ST YEAR LAW STUDENT
I INTEND TO USE LAW TO FIGHT POVERTY AND INJUSTICE
2ND YEAR LAW STUDENT
...BUT MAYBE I CAN DO SOME CORPORATE WORK ON THE SIDE...
...WHILE I HELP OUT AT THE FREE REPRES-ENTATION UNIT.
FINAL YEAR LAW STUDENT
FIRST I'LL MAKE A PILE OF MONEY
...THEN I'LL SAVE THE WORLD...
LAW FIRM ASSOCIATE
I CAN'T BELIEVE MY STINGY FIRM EXPECTS ME TO LIVE ON £60K A YEAR.
THIS IS POVERTY AND INJUSTICE
LAW FIRM PARTNER
OF COURSE YOU CAN DO PRO BONO WORK... AS LONG AS THE FIRM HAS NO FEE-PAYING WORK TO BE DONE FIRST
SHAME

BAR STUDENTS, LOOK TO THE PERSON SITTING TO YOUR RIGHT, AND TO YOUR LEFT.
ONLY ONE IN THREE OF YOU WILL FIND A PUPILLAGE AT THE BAR.
I'LL BE THAT ONE...
OF THE REMAINDER, JUST ONE IN FIVE WILL FIND A TENANCY.
I'LL BE THAT ONE...
OF THE REST, ONE IN TEN WILL STILL BE IN PRACTICE IN TEN YEARS.
I'LL BE THAT ONE...
...AND ONE IN A MILLION WILL STILL REMEMBER, AT THE END OF YOUR CAREERS, WHY YOU WENT INTO LAW IN THE FIRST PLACE.

LAW SCHOOL LECTURERS
PROFESSOR VANITY
THIS IS YOUR VITAL TEXT-BOOK. ...BY ME, OF COURSE.
THE RUIN
(HAS GIVEN THE SAME LECTURE FOR 30 YEARS.)
THE TERRORIST
EVERY SINGLE ONE OF YOU WILL FAIL YOUR FINALS!
I HATE MY LIFE...
MR PERFECT *
LET ME SUGGEST SOME AREAS OF REVISION FOR NEXT WEEK'S EXAM.
WINK!
*WARNING: VERY RARE

LAW STUDENTS - a USER'S GUIDE:
① MR SWAGGER
I'VE GOT SEVEN INTER-VIEWS NEXT WEEK.
FAKE TAN
HOW ABOUT YOU?
INVESTOR'S CHRONICLE
② MISS TERRIFIED.
HAVE YOU READ ALL THE TEXT BOOKS?
IS YOUR APPLICATION IN?
DID YOU DO THE HOME-WORK?
IS IT TOO LATE?
AIR OF PANIC
③ MR CONFUSED.
BARRISTER, SOLICITOR, ...OR ACCOUNTANT?
OR SHOULD I GO TO MEDICAL SCHOOL INSTEAD?
www.qccartoon.com
④ MISS PERFECT.*
DON'T WORRY - YOU CAN READ MY ESSAY.
SHARING ISN'T CHEATING!
...AND HERE ARE LAST WEEK'S NOTES.
* WARNING: VERY RARE

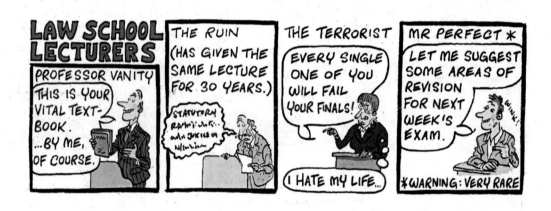

LAW EXAMINATION QUESTION ONE:
IF JOHN DOE BEQUEATHS HIS ESTATE POUR AUTRE VIE TO HIS LEGATEE RICHARD ROE...
TICK TICK
HOW DOES THE CONVERSION AD PERSONAM AFFECT THE CHOSE IN ACTION OF THE EXPECTANT ASSIGNEE?
TICK TICK
DISCUSS IN THE LIGHT OF THE DOCTRINE OF SUBROGATION AND THE YORK-ANTWERP CONVENTION.
TICK TICK
TICK TICK
I'VE CHANGED MY MIND. I THINK I'M GOING TO BE A DOCTOR INSTEAD.

COLLEGE OF LAW
WHEN DO YOU START YOUR TRAINING CONTRACT WITH YOUR NEW FIRM?
OH... THEY'VE DEFERRED ME A YEAR SINCE BUSINESS IS SO SLOW...
MEANWHILE I'M TO USE THE TIME PRODUCTIVELY... DEVELOP SKILLS I WILL NEED WHEN I QUALIFY AS A SOLICITOR.
LIKE WHAT, EXACTLY?
ER ... DUNNO. TRAVEL AROUND EUROPE I SUPPOSE. I'LL THINK OF SOMETHING.
GENTLEMEN... PLACE YOUR BETS.
CASINO

LAW GRADUATES OF 1999, IT IS AN HONOURABLE CALLING YOU HAVE CHOSEN.
SCHOOL OF LAW
SOME OF YOU ARE DESTINED TO DEFEND POOR HELPLESS INSURANCE COMPANIES AGAINST GREEDY CAR CRASH VICTIMS TRYING TO CLAIM FOR THEIR INJURIES.
SCHOOL OF LAW
OTHERS WILL TOIL TO PROTECT BELEAGUERED TOBACCO MULTINATIONALS FROM ATTACK BY EXTREMIST CONSUMER GROUPS.
SCHOOL OF LAW
REMEMBER ... SPEAK LOUDLY AND DEMAND A BIG RETAINER.
SCHOOL

GRADUATING CLASS OF 1999, I CONGRATULATE YOU ALL.
COLLEGE OF LAW
THREE YEARS AGO, WHEN ASKED A LEGAL QUESTION, YOU COULD ANSWER IN ALL HONESTY: "I DON'T KNOW".
NOW, YOU CAN SAY WITH ALL THE AUTHORITY YOU CAN MUSTER...
COLLEGE OF LAW
...IT DEPENDS
COLLEGE OF LAW

SKILLS THEY DON'T TEACH YOU IN LAW SCHOOL (BUT SHOULD)
HOW TO EXPLAIN TO YOUR CLIENT (WHO IS PAYING £300 AN HOUR) WHY YOU LOST HIS CASE
GRRRR!
HOW TO FIX THE PHOTOCOPIER AT 3am ARMED ONLY WITH A COAT HANGER AND A STAPLE GUN
AAAAAARG!
FIRE AXE
JAMMED
HOW TO CONCEAL FROM YOUR COLLEAGUES THAT YOUR SECRETARY KNOWS TEN TIMES AS MUCH LAW AS YOU DO.
HERE YOU ARE DEAR, ...LET ME SHOW YOU HOW IT'S DONE.
SHAME
HOW TO BOOK YOUR HOLIDAY 6 MONTHS AHEAD ...AND CANCEL IT THE DAY BEFORE
URGENT CASE... ALL HOLIDAYS SUSPENDED
HOW TO ADOPT A LOOK OF RAPT FASCINATION AS THE SENIOR PARTNER TELLS YOU ABOUT HIS LATEST CASE.
BLAH BLAH
ZZ

QUESTION FOR YOU, HELENA: A RICH MAN DIES, LEAVING NO WILL. WHICH OF HIS RELATIVES GETS THE MONEY?
ER... I DON'T KNOW.
NONE OF THEM! DON'T THEY TEACH YOU ANYTHING AT LAW SCHOOL?
WELL... WHO DOES GET THE MONEY THEN?
WE DO.

LEGAL SKILLS THEY OUGHT TO TEACH IN LAW SCHOOL BUT DON'T:
① TIME SHEET PADDING
HMMM... I WONDER IF I CAN CLAIM BATHROOM TIME...
② BRINGING IN NEW CLIENTS (AND WATCHING THE SENIOR PARTNER TAKE CREDIT)
SHAKE
③ LOSING CLIENTS, ...THROUGH NO FAULT OF YOUR OWN... (AND TAKING THE BLAME)
MEA CULPA
④ KEEPING UP WITH FIRM POLITICS
YOU ASKED THAT IDIOT FOR ADVICE ON MY CASE!?
SHAME
FINDING NON-EXISTENT CASE LAW TO SUPPORT FRIVOLOUS CLAIMS.
WHAT DO YOU MEAN "IT DOESN'T EXIST"?!? YOU'RE NOT LOOKING HARD ENOUGH!!

I SOMETIMES WONDER WHY I BOTHERED GOING TO LAW SCHOOL.
NOW THAT I HAVE A JOB, IT'S ALL LONG HOURS AND HIGH STRESS.
...PLUS HARDLY ANY CHANCE OF PARTNERSHIP!
...YOU WANT FRIES WITH THAT?
YEAH...
...AND A MILKSHAKE.

SOMETIMES I GET SO FED UP WITH BEING A LAWYER.
THE LONG HOURS, THE UNGRATEFUL CLIENTS,
THE STRESS, THE ENDLESS WORRY, THE GRUMPY PARTNERS...
...BUT THEN I REMEMBER WHY I WENT INTO LAW IN THE FIRST PLACE...
...TO PAY OFF MY STUDENT LOANS.

the LAW SCHOOL REUNION
OH... HELLO!
HI!
WHO ARE YOU?
...WHAT'S YOUR NAME?
YOU LOOK GREAT!
YOU TOO!
SO OLD! AND TIRED!
HOW ARE YOU DOING?
ARE YOU MORE SUCCESSFUL THAN ME?
I'M A PARTNER IN A CITY LAW FIRM.
I'VE JUST TAKEN SILK
BASTARD
DAMN.

WELL, TODAY IS THE THIRTIETH ANNIVERSARY OF MY JOINING THE FIRM.
BAR
WHAT DO YOU HAVE THERE? A LETTER OF CONGRATULATIONS?
NO, EVEN BETTER.
FULL EQUITY PARTNERSHIP?
BETTER THAN THAT.
A GOLD WATCH?
BETTER.
...A LETTER FROM MY BANK SAYING I'VE FINALLY PAID OFF MY STUDENT LOANS.

THE LAWYER'S PROGRESS
www.qccartoon.com

CHAPTER TWO
PUPILLAGE

You'll find we're one big happy family here

YOU HAVE SIX A-STARS AT A-LEVEL, A FIRST CLASS DEGREE, AND YOU ARE TOP OF YOUR CLASS AT LAW SCHOOL
YOU DO PRO BONO WORK, HELP OUT AT THE LAW CENTRE, AND YOU'RE THE ALL-ENGLAND DEBATING CHAMPION
COMPETITION FOR A PUPILLAGE AT THESE CHAMBERS IS VERY FIERCE THIS YEAR.
... WE'RE REALLY LOOKING FOR SOMEONE WHO'S A BIT MORE OF A HIGH ACHIEVER.

I SEE FROM YOUR CV THAT YOU WERE ROWING CAPTAIN AT UNIVERSITY, PLUS YOU WON MEDALS FOR FOOTBALL, RUGBY AND ATHLETICS.
YES
WELL, WE COULD USE A STRONG CHAP LIKE YOU TO SHOULDER SOME HEAVY RESPONSIBILITY AROUND HERE.
WE'D LIKE TO OFFER YOU A PUPILLAGE.
WELCOME ABOARD
HURRY UP WITH THOSE FILES. WE MUSTN'T KEEP SIR GEOFFREY WAITING.

HOW ARE THE PUPILLAGE CANDIDATES THIS YEAR?
EXCELLENT. THE LAST ONE WAS ESPECIALLY IMPRESSIVE.
HE WORE A WELL-TAILORED SUIT, FOUR BUTTONS ON EACH CUFF, TWO SIDE VENTS AND A DARK CHARCOAL STRIPE.
WELTED HALF-BROGUES AND A DOUBLE-CUFFED SHIRT.
ER... AND HIS ACADEMIC RECORD?
...DIDN'T REALLY NOTICE. BUT I'M SURE HE'LL FIT RIGHT IN.

AS A PUPIL BARRISTER YOUR JOB IS TO REMAIN SILENT AT ALL TIMES. NEVER SPEAK UNTIL SPOKEN TO.
NEVER LOOK A SENIOR MEMBER OF CHAMBERS IN THE EYE. AND NEVER TALK DURING CHAMBERS' TEA.
IN FACT... BE COMPLETELY INVISIBLE. BUT, MOST IMPORTANT OF ALL...
...TRY TO HAVE FUN. IN THE END, THAT'S WHAT IT'S ALL ABOUT.

AS A LEADING COMMERCIAL SET OF CHAMBERS, IT IS VITAL THAT WE SELECT PUPILS WITH THE FINEST QUALIFICATIONS.
ONLY THE BEST-SUITED CANDIDATES WILL SUCCEED.
...SO I MUST ASK YOU ONE VITAL QUESTION.
WHAT FOOTBALL TEAM DO YOU SUPPORT?
SPURS.
EXCELLENT. YOU'RE IN.

MARK UP THESE PAPERS FOR ME WOULD YOU, CRAWLEY?
ER... WHAT POINTS SHOULD I FOCUS ON?
NONE AT ALL. JUST MARK THE PAGES UP RANDOMLY IN RED INK, LIKE THIS.
BUT WHY WOULD I JUST MARK THE PAGES UP RANDOMLY?
BECAUSE...
THE CASE SETTLED THIS MORNING, AND I NEED TO CONVINCE MY SOLICITORS THAT MY ENORMOUS BRIEF FEE IS JUSTIFIED.

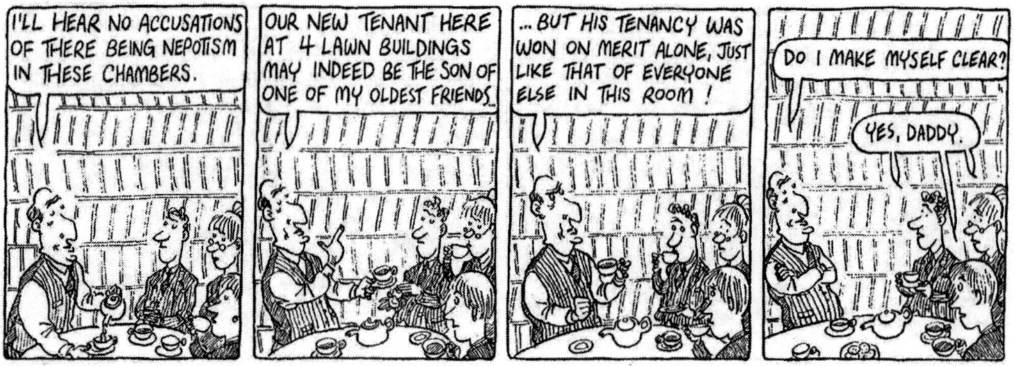
I'LL HEAR NO ACCUSATIONS OF THERE BEING NEPOTISM IN THESE CHAMBERS.
OUR NEW TENANT HERE AT 4 LAWN BUILDINGS MAY INDEED BE THE SON OF ONE OF MY OLDEST FRIENDS...
... BUT HIS TENANCY WAS WON ON MERIT ALONE, JUST LIKE THAT OF EVERYONE ELSE IN THIS ROOM!
DO I MAKE MYSELF CLEAR?
YES, DADDY.

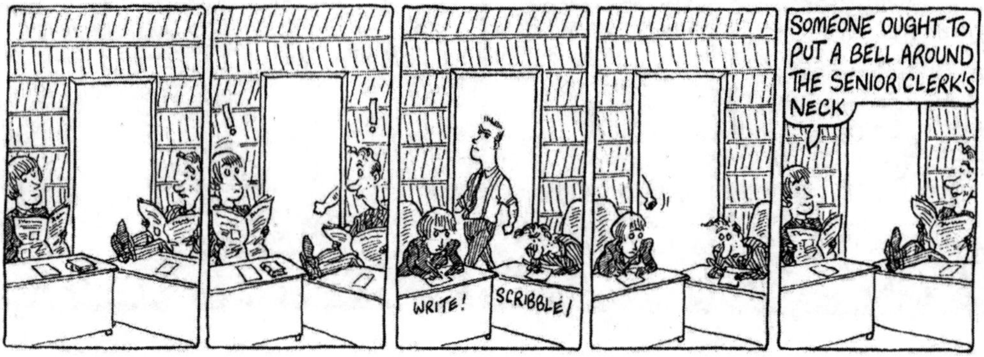
WRITE!
SCRIBBLE!
SOMEONE OUGHT TO PUT A BELL AROUND THE SENIOR CLERK'S NECK

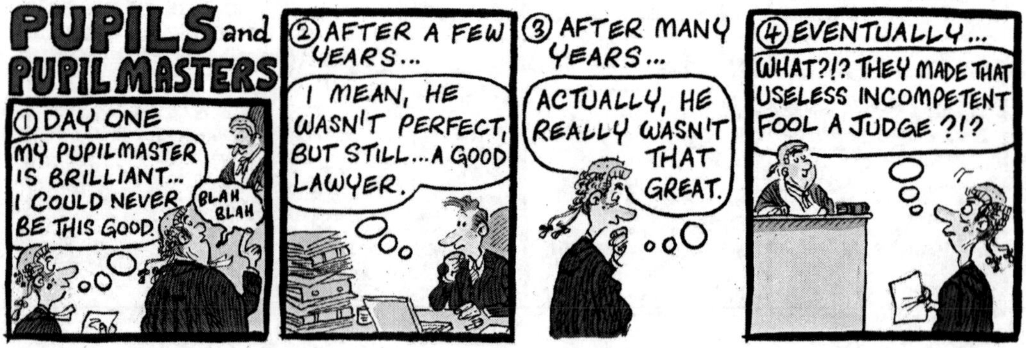
PUPILS and PUPIL MASTERS
① DAY ONE
MY PUPILMASTER IS BRILLIANT... I COULD NEVER BE THIS GOOD.
BLAH BLAH
② AFTER A FEW YEARS...
I MEAN, HE WASN'T PERFECT, BUT STILL... A GOOD LAWYER.
③ AFTER MANY YEARS...
ACTUALLY, HE REALLY WASN'T THAT GREAT.
④ EVENTUALLY...
WHAT?!? THEY MADE THAT USELESS INCOMPETENT FOOL A JUDGE ?!?

OH DEAR, HELENA'S OVERDOING IT A BIT AT THE CHRISTMAS PARTY.
DEFINITELY ONE OVER THE DOZEN.
OH NO... SIR GEOFFREY'S MOVING IN... !
HE'S TAKING ADVANTAGE!
HE'S WHISPERING SOMETHING TO HER!
WHAT'S HE SAYING?
MM...YES...
GENTLEMEN... HELENA HAS AGREED TO TAKE OVER THE RUNNING OF CHAMBERS LIBRARY.
OH NO!
SHE'LL REGRET THAT IN THE MORNING.

SO I FINALLY STOOD UP TO THE CLERKS! TWO WEEKS AGO I REALLY TOLD THEM WHO'S BOSS!
OH?
I SAID "NO MORE CRAPPY BRIEFS FOR LOW PAY. JUST SEND ME THE GOOD STUFF!"
GOOD FOR YOU
AND DID IT WORK?
ABSOLUTELY!
SINCE THEN THEY HAVEN'T SENT ME A SINGLE BRIEF!

MR SPROCKET, SIR GEOFFREY WILL EXPLAIN YOUR CASE TO YOU...
...AS I HAVEN'T READ THE PAPERS...
!
...BUT I'VE HARDLY LOOKED AT THIS...
ER... I THINK I'LL LET MY JUNIOR OPEN THIS ONE...
WHAT? NOT ME... !?!
ER... ACTUALLY...
...THE PERSON WITH THE BEST GRASP OF THE DETAIL...
...IS MY PUPIL, CRAWLEY. HE'LL EXPLAIN IT ALL WON'T YOU?
ER, UM...
HELP!

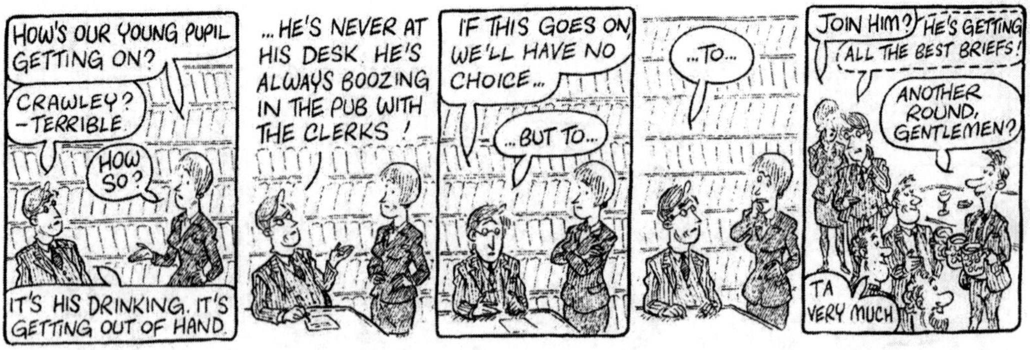
HOW'S OUR YOUNG PUPIL GETTING ON?
CRAWLEY? -TERRIBLE
HOW SO?
IT'S HIS DRINKING. IT'S GETTING OUT OF HAND.
... HE'S NEVER AT HIS DESK. HE'S ALWAYS BOOZING IN THE PUB WITH THE CLERKS!
IF THIS GOES ON, WE'LL HAVE NO CHOICE...
... BUT TO...
... TO...
JOIN HIM?
HE'S GETTING ALL THE BEST BRIEFS!
ANOTHER ROUND, GENTLEMEN?
TA VERY MUCH

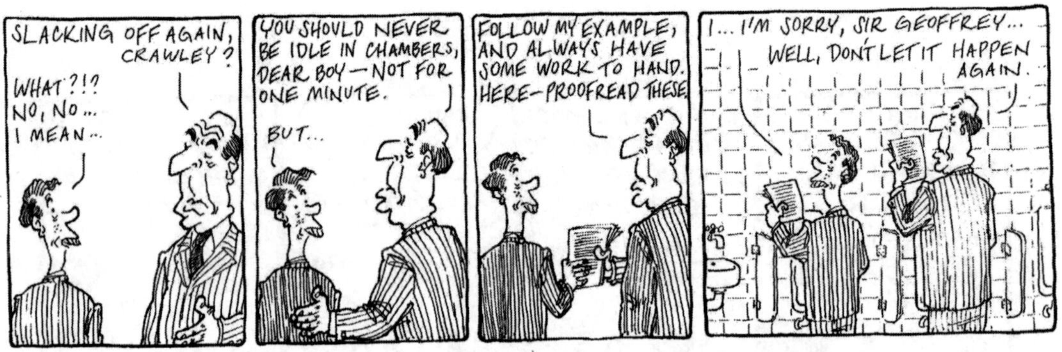
SLACKING OFF AGAIN, CRAWLEY?
WHAT?!? NO, NO... I MEAN...
YOU SHOULD NEVER BE IDLE IN CHAMBERS, DEAR BOY — NOT FOR ONE MINUTE.
BUT...
FOLLOW MY EXAMPLE, AND ALWAYS HAVE SOME WORK TO HAND. HERE— PROOFREAD THESE.
I... I'M SORRY, SIR GEOFFREY...
WELL, DON'T LET IT HAPPEN AGAIN.

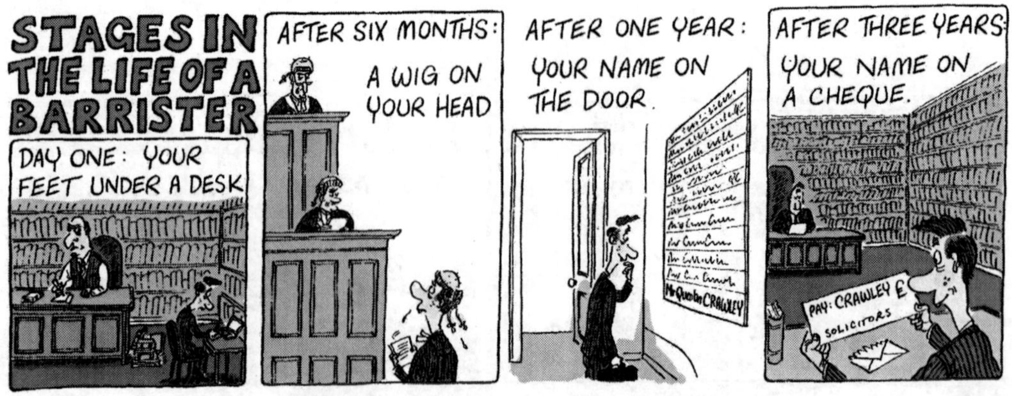
STAGES IN THE LIFE OF A BARRISTER
DAY ONE: YOUR FEET UNDER A DESK
AFTER SIX MONTHS: A WIG ON YOUR HEAD
AFTER ONE YEAR: YOUR NAME ON THE DOOR.
Mr Quentin CRAWLEY
AFTER THREE YEARS: YOUR NAME ON A CHEQUE.
PAY: CRAWLEY £
SOLICITORS

SO WHAT MADE YOU WANT TO BE A JUDGE, HUMPHREY?
TO HELP THE UNFORTUNATE!
INDEED?
YES, THE POOR, THE DOWNTRODDEN. THOSE POOR CREATURES WHO NEVER GET A BREAK!
YOU MEAN... VICTIMS OF CRIME?
OH NO!
PUPIL BARRISTERS! ... RELEASED INTO COURT FOR THE FIRST TIME
ER... YOUR HONOUR... I MEAN, M'LUD...
TREMBLE
NOW, MR CRAWLEY, TAKE A DEEP BREATH AND START AGAIN...

IF THE LAW IS ON YOUR SIDE, ARGUE THE LAW.
IF THE FACTS ARE ON YOUR SIDE, ARGUE THE FACTS.
...BUT WHAT IF NEITHER THE LAW NOR THE FACTS ARE ON YOUR SIDE?
TELL THE JUDGE IT'S A QUESTION OF HUMAN RIGHTS.

the BARRISTER'S PROGRESS
① THE PUPIL.
WHY CAN'T CHAMBERS TAKE ON MORE PUPILS? THERE'S PLENTY OF WORK FOR US ALL.
② JUNIOR TENANT
AT LAST THEY RECOGNISED MY TALENT AND INVITED ME TO JOIN CHAMBERS.
③ TWO YEAR'S CALL
WHY ARE THEY TAKING ON MORE PUPILS? THE GREEDY SQUIRTS WILL TAKE ALL MY WORK.
④ TEN YEAR'S CALL
I CAN'T BELIEVE I HAVE TO TAKE ON A PUPIL AND SHOW HIM THE ROPES. WHAT AM I – A NANNY?

IT'S ABOUT TIME CHAMBERS DECIDED WHICH OF OUR PUPILS TO KEEP ON THIS YEAR.
WELL, CRAWLEY'S PAPERWORK IS GOOD, BUT HELENA IS A BETTER ADVOCATE...
...AND SHE'S BETTER LOOKING!
HONESTLY, SIR GEOFFREY!
WE MUST BE SCIENTIFIC ABOUT THIS — APPLY PROPER SELECTION PROCEDURES AND EVALUATE THEIR SKILLS.
OH, ALRIGHT THEN.
LET'S SEE WHICH ONE GETS THE MOST RUNS.
4 LAWN BUILDINGS CRICKET MATCH
AGREED.

SO LET'S SEE... WHO'S UP FOR TENANCY IN CHAMBERS THIS YEAR? I HEAR HELENA'S PAPERWORK IS GOOD.
FLAWLESS.
MARVELLOUS ADVOCATE, TOO
I'D SAY SHE'S THE MOST PROMISING PUPIL CHAMBERS HAS HAD IN YEARS.
WITHOUT A DOUBT
I SEE. HIGH PRAISE INDEED.
...WELL THAT LEAVES US WITH NO CHOICE THEN, DOES IT?
NOT REALLY.
WE'LL HAVE TO GET RID OF HER.
...CAN'T HAVE HER MAKING US LOOK BAD.
—PINCHING OUR WORK

WHAT DO YOU THINK OF THIS ONE?
BETTER THAN LAST YEAR'S.
DELICIOUS.
FULL-BODIED.
GOOD NOSE, TOO.
..MMM
WELL-ROUNDED CHARACTER.
UNPRETENTIOUS.
?
IN FACT, WE THINK YOU'VE MADE AN EXCELLENT PUPIL BARRISTER, HELENA.
...WE'D LIKE YOU TO STAY ON FOR ANOTHER SIX MONTHS.

CHAPTER THREE
JUNIOR BAR

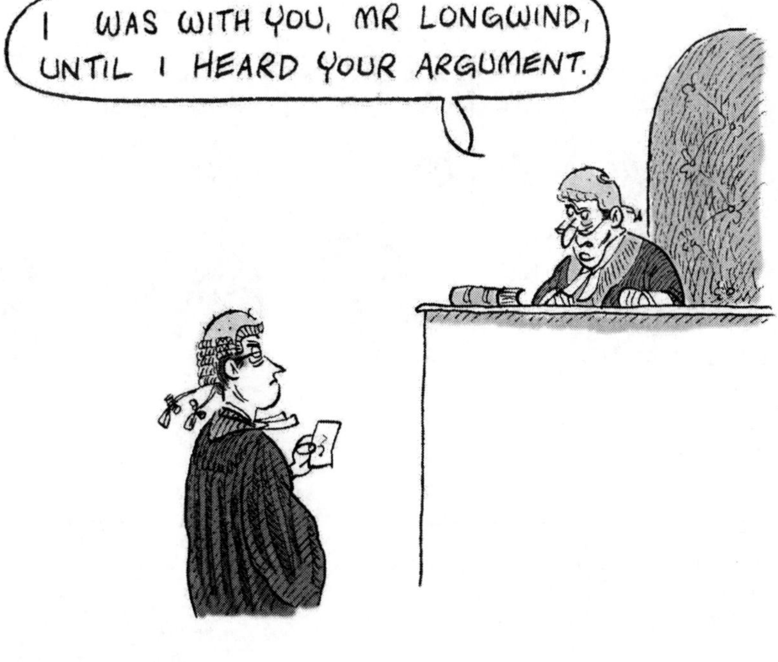
I WAS WITH YOU, MR LONGWIND, UNTIL I HEARD YOUR ARGUMENT.

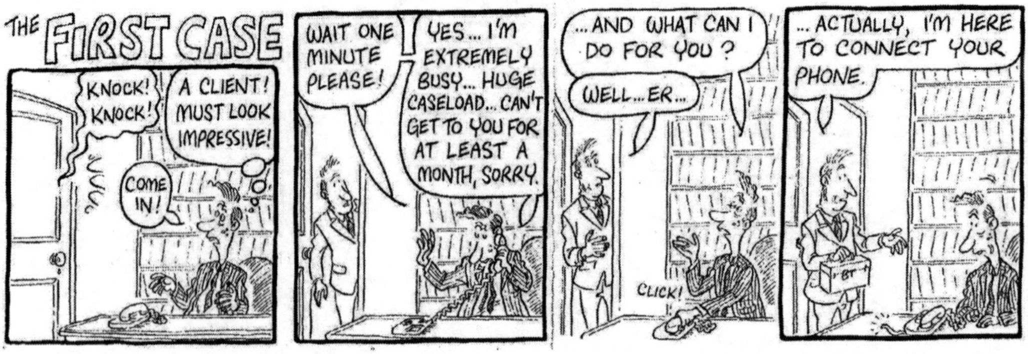
THE FIRST CASE
KNOCK! KNOCK!
A CLIENT! MUST LOOK IMPRESSIVE!
COME IN!
WAIT ONE MINUTE PLEASE!
YES... I'M EXTREMELY BUSY... HUGE CASELOAD... CAN'T GET TO YOU FOR AT LEAST A MONTH, SORRY.
...AND WHAT CAN I DO FOR YOU ?
WELL... ER...
CLICK!
... ACTUALLY, I'M HERE TO CONNECT YOUR PHONE.
BT

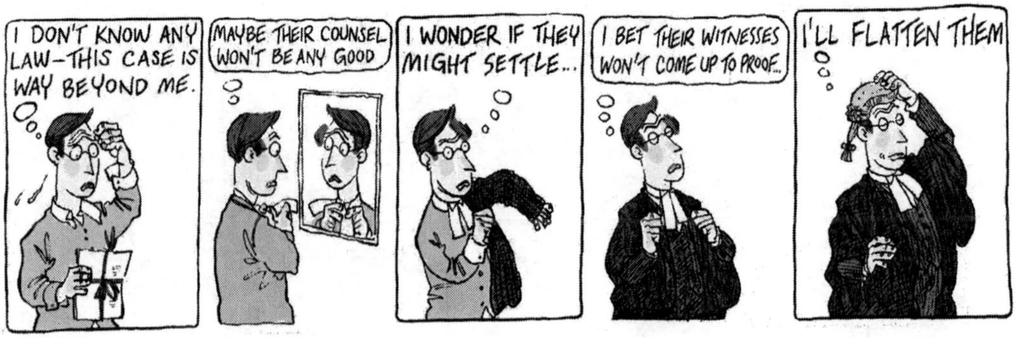
I DON'T KNOW ANY LAW—THIS CASE IS WAY BEYOND ME.
MAYBE THEIR COUNSEL WON'T BE ANY GOOD
I WONDER IF THEY MIGHT SETTLE...
I BET THEIR WITNESSES WON'T COME UP TO PROOF...
I'LL FLATTEN THEM

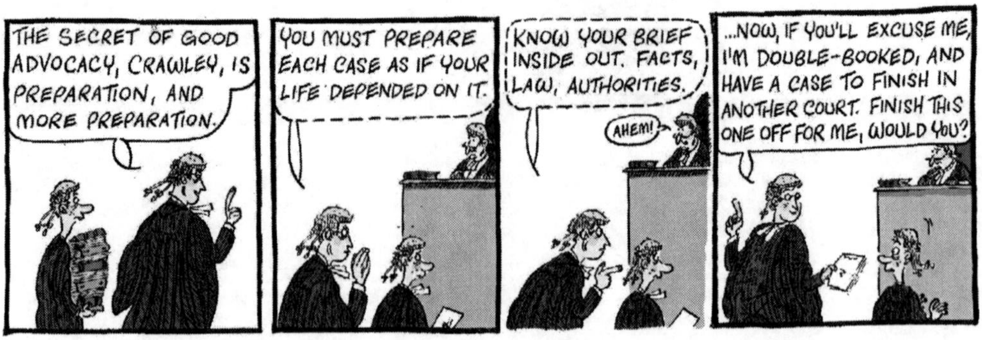
THE SECRET OF GOOD ADVOCACY, CRAWLEY, IS PREPARATION, AND MORE PREPARATION.
YOU MUST PREPARE EACH CASE AS IF YOUR LIFE DEPENDED ON IT.
KNOW YOUR BRIEF INSIDE OUT. FACTS, LAW, AUTHORITIES.
AHEM!
...NOW, IF YOU'LL EXCUSE ME, I'M DOUBLE-BOOKED, AND HAVE A CASE TO FINISH IN ANOTHER COURT. FINISH THIS ONE OFF FOR ME, WOULD YOU?

EDWARD, AS JUNIOR COUNSEL, YOUR EXPERTISE WILL BE INVALUABLE IN THIS CASE.
I'VE GOT NO IDEA WHAT I'M DOING
I KNOW YOU WON'T MIND TAKING SOME OF THE TRICKIER LEGAL POINTS.
I'VE FORGOTTEN THE LAW ON THIS.
WE WILL NEED TO PLAN A CAREFUL DISTRIBUTION OF WORK.
...SO THAT YOU DO ALL OF IT...
...AND, AS LEADING COUNSEL, I GET TO TAKE ALL THE CREDIT.
CLICK!
FLASH!
TODAY'S JUDGEMENT IS A HISTORIC VICTORY...

OFFICER, WHEN YOU FIRST SAW MY CLIENT, HE HAD CROSSED THE CENTRE LINE, SO YOU PULLED HIM OVER?
YES.
...AND YOU SMELLED ALCOHOL ON HIS BREATH?
YES
BUT APART FROM THAT, WAS THERE ANY EVIDENCE THAT HE WAS DRIVING UNDER THE INFLUENCE OF ALCOHOL?
WELL...
HE WASN'T WEARING ANY TROUSERS AND HIS BOXER SHORTS WERE ON HIS HEAD.
CRAWLEY DEAR BOY, NEVER ASK THE WITNESS A QUESTION TO WHICH YOU DON'T ALREADY KNOW THE ANSWER.

BIG CASE FOR YOU MR CRAWLEY. THREE WEEKS IN THE HIGH COURT
REALLY, DEREK?
...BOUND TO GO TO THE COURT OF APPEAL AND THE HOUSE OF LORDS.
OH... AND YOUR FEE IS TO BE PAID IN ADVANCE
RUB
ER... MR CRAWLEY?
WHA...?
KNOCK!
POOF!
BRIEF FOR YOU TOMORROW, SIR. SHOREDITCH MAGISTRATES' COURT, 8.30 AM. LEGAL AID, NO EXPENSES

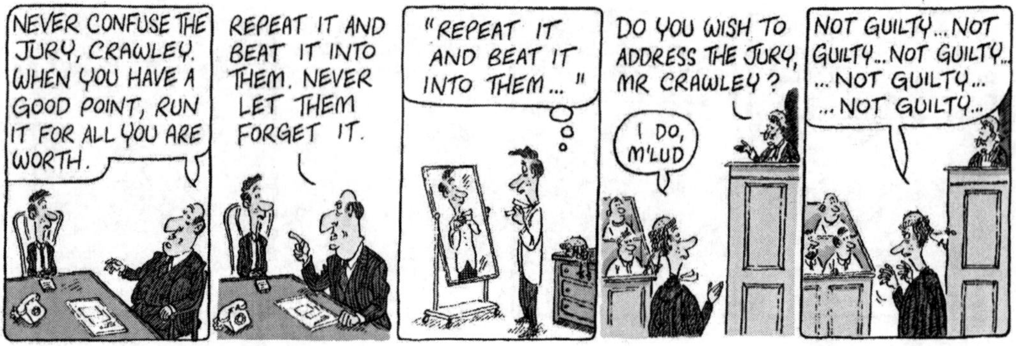
NEVER CONFUSE THE JURY, CRAWLEY. WHEN YOU HAVE A GOOD POINT, RUN IT FOR ALL YOU ARE WORTH.
REPEAT IT AND BEAT IT INTO THEM. NEVER LET THEM FORGET IT.
"REPEAT IT AND BEAT IT INTO THEM..."
DO YOU WISH TO ADDRESS THE JURY, MR CRAWLEY?
I DO, M'LUD
NOT GUILTY... NOT GUILTY... NOT GUILTY... ...NOT GUILTY... ...NOT GUILTY...

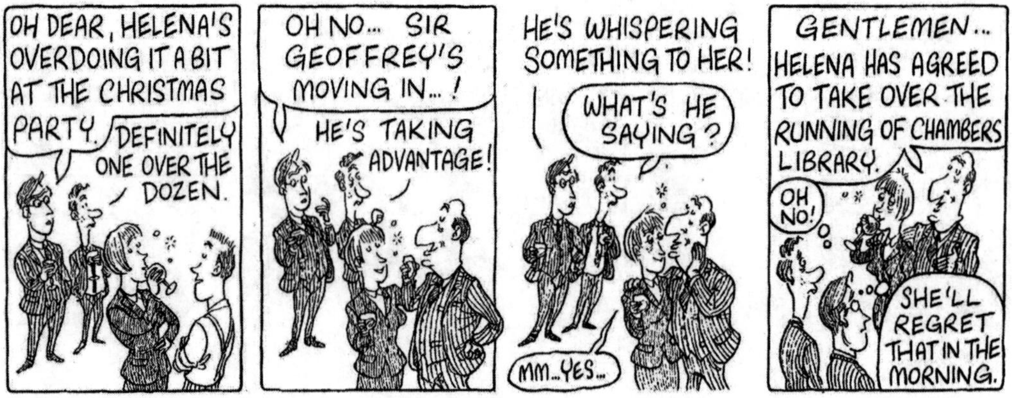
OH DEAR, HELENA'S OVERDOING IT A BIT AT THE CHRISTMAS PARTY.
DEFINITELY ONE OVER THE DOZEN.
OH NO... SIR GEOFFREY'S MOVING IN...!
HE'S TAKING ADVANTAGE!
HE'S WHISPERING SOMETHING TO HER!
WHAT'S HE SAYING?
MM...YES...
GENTLEMEN... HELENA HAS AGREED TO TAKE OVER THE RUNNING OF CHAMBERS LIBRARY.
OH NO!
SHE'LL REGRET THAT IN THE MORNING.

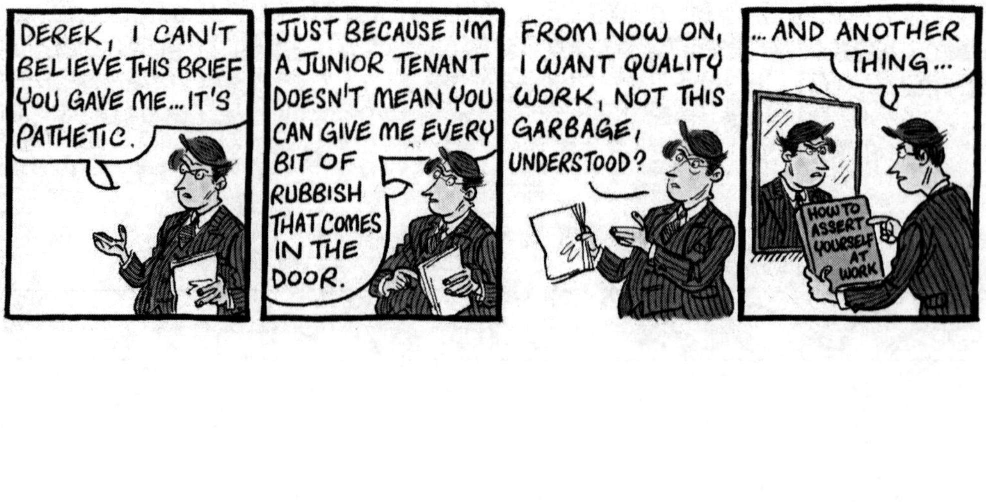
DEREK, I CAN'T BELIEVE THIS BRIEF YOU GAVE ME... IT'S PATHETIC.
JUST BECAUSE I'M A JUNIOR TENANT DOESN'T MEAN YOU CAN GIVE ME EVERY BIT OF RUBBISH THAT COMES IN THE DOOR.
FROM NOW ON, I WANT QUALITY WORK, NOT THIS GARBAGE, UNDERSTOOD?
...AND ANOTHER THING...
HOW TO ASSERT YOURSELF AT WORK

THIS IS TOO COMPLICATED, DEAR. WE NEED TO SEE AN EXPERT SOLICITOR.
THIS IS A VERY COMPLEX CASE, MR SPROCKETT. WE NEED TO INSTRUCT EXPERT COUNSEL.
YOU'LL DEFINITELY NEED AN EXPERT BARRISTER FOR THIS ONE, MR LOOPHOLE.
SENIOR CLERK
YOUR BRIEF, MR LONGWIND.
THANKS, DEREK
SENIOR CLERK
HELLO... SAM? I'VE NEVER DONE ONE OF THESE BEFORE. GOT ANY TIPS?

OI MATE, HAND OVER YOUR WALLET!
!
ALRIGHT... BUT WAIT... DON'T I KNOW YOU?
YOU'RE MY CLIENT! WHAT SORT OF CLIENT MUGS HIS OWN LAWYER?
THE ONE YOU FAILED TO GET OFF.
OH.

I'VE HAD ENOUGH OF THESE RUBBISH BRIEFS FROM THE CLERKS.
PATHETIC CASES...
NO MONEY AT ALL!
I'M GOING TO TALK TO THE HEAD CLERK, AND SHOW HIM WHO'S BOSS!
DEREK?
MR CRAWLEY SIR... HOW CAN I HELP YOU?
ER... MAY I SAY HOW VERY MUCH THAT TIE SUITS YOU?
THANKYOU SIR

OH YES, LOTS OF WORK, MUM. THE BRIEFS JUST FLOOD IN.
...HARDLY A LET-UP REALLY. IT'S ONE CASE AFTER ANOTHER.
MUST DASH. THAT'LL BE ONE OF MY CLIENTS NOW.
KNOCK! KNOCK!
SIGH!
WHHIRRRR

THERE ARE TOO MANY CASES LISTED, MR SPROCKET, SO THE COURT CAN'T HEAR YOURS TODAY.
I'M AFRAID WE'VE ALL HAD A WASTED MORNING, AND WE'LL HAVE TO GO HOME EARLY.
IT ALSO MEANS INCREASED COSTS, UNFORTUNATELY.
IT'S REALLY VERY FRUSTRATING– I'M VERY SORRY INDEED.
YIPPEE!

I'M SO SORRY I'M LATE, RICHARD — MY CLERK SENT ME TO THE WRONG COURT.
THIS TIME DEREK'S GONE TOO FAR. I'LL REALLY GIVE HIM A ROCKET FOR THIS.
SURELY YOU CAN'T AFFORD TO ANNOY YOUR SENIOR CLERK, EDWARD? DOESN'T HE CONTROL YOUR CAREER?
HMF!
SOMETIMES THE CLERKS NEED REMINDING WHO IS THE BOSS IN CHAMBERS.
GOOD DAY IN COURT, MR LONG-WIND?
OH, EXCELLENT, DEREK. ANYTHING INTERESTING FOR ME TOMORROW?

CRAWLEY, THE GREAT THING ABOUT A CAREER AT THE BAR IS THE FREEDOM IT GIVES YOU.
WE BARRISTERS ARE THE LAST TRULY INDEPENDENT PROFESSIONALS.
4 LAWN BLDGS
...UNLIKE SOLICITORS, WE TAKE ORDERS FROM NO-ONE.
CLERK'S ROOM
BRIEF FOR YOU, SIR. 8AM, PENZANCE MAGISTRATES, LEGAL AID, NO EXPENSES
ER, THANKYOU DEREK.
...EXCEPT FROM YOUR CLERK, OF COURSE...

WE SHOULD SETTLE THIS CASE. MY SIDE IS BOUND TO WIN TODAY.
YOUR CLAIM ISN'T NEARLY AS STRONG AS YOU THINK.
VERY IFFY, IN FACT.
ER, NOW LOOK HERE OLD CHAP...
I'VE GOT A VERY LUCRATIVE BRIEF IN THE HIGH COURT TOMORROW, AND I'LL HAVE TO PASS IT UP IF THIS CASE GOES AHEAD.
ME TOO... LET'S SETTLE

QUESTION FOR YOU, HELENA: A RICH MAN DIES, LEAVING NO WILL. WHICH OF HIS RELATIVES GETS THE MONEY?
ER... I DON'T KNOW.
NONE OF THEM! DON'T THEY TEACH YOU ANYTHING AT LAW SCHOOL?
WELL... WHO DOES GET THE MONEY THEN?
WE DO.

STOP! THIEF! MY HANDBAG! THIEF!
QUICK OFFICER! HE WENT THAT WAY!
STOP THIEF!
MY CARD, YOUNG MAN, IN CASE THEY CATCH YOU.

RATHER TIED UP AT THE MOMENT, YES... BIG CASE IN THE HOUSE OF LORDS...
GLOBAL SIGNIF-ICANCE...
VERY IMPORTANT... LOOK, I REALLY CAN'T FIT YOU IN RIGHT NOW.
YOU'LL HAVE TO SPEAK TO THE CLERKS, THEY'LL SORT YOU OUT WITH AN APPOINTMENT IN A FEW WEEKS.
'BYE MUM.

THE QUEEN'S COUNSEL SYSTEM IS OUTMODED AND OUTDATED. IT'S JUST AN EXCUSE TO CHARGE HUGE FEES!
...ARCHAIC, ELITIST AND A CONSPIRACY AGAINST THE PUBLIC!
THE WHOLE THING SHOULD BE ABOLISHED.
...SO YOU GOT TURNED DOWN AGAIN THEN?
HOW DID YOU KNOW?

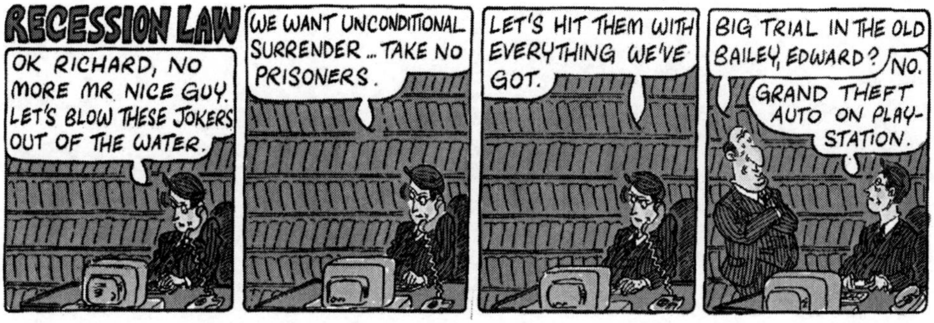
RECESSION LAW
OK RICHARD, NO MORE MR. NICE GUY. LET'S BLOW THESE JOKERS OUT OF THE WATER.
WE WANT UNCONDITIONAL SURRENDER ... TAKE NO PRISONERS.
LET'S HIT THEM WITH EVERYTHING WE'VE GOT.
BIG TRIAL IN THE OLD BAILEY, EDWARD?
NO. GRAND THEFT AUTO ON PLAY-STATION.

CHAPTER FOUR
QUEEN'S COUNSEL

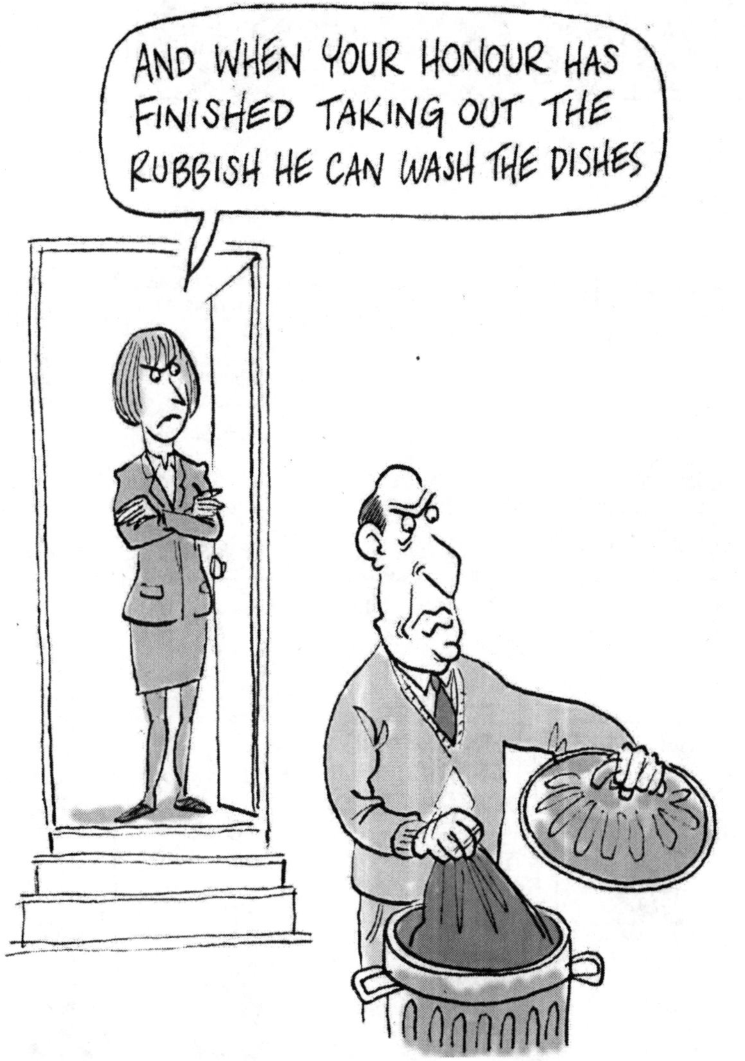
AND WHEN YOUR HONOUR HAS FINISHED TAKING OUT THE RUBBISH HE CAN WASH THE DISHES

WHAT DO YOU MAKE OF THAT CHAP WATKINS? HE'S A PRETTY GOOD LAWYER, ISN'T HE?
"PIGGY" WATKINS? EVERYONE USED TO TEASE HIM AT SCHOOL.
AND GUESS WHAT I HEARD ON THE GRAPEVINE... *WHISPER*
REALLY?
HA! HA! HA!
HO! HO! HO!
LORD CHANCELLOR'S DEPARTMENT
WELL, WE DEFINITELY SHAN'T MAKE HIM A QC.
CERTAINLY NOT.
NO ENTRY QC SELECTION PANEL SITTING

PRIMA FACIE, MR SPROCKET, THIS IS A CASE OF RES IPSA LOQUITUR.
HOWEVER, MUTATIS MUTANDIS, THERE IS, IPSO FACTO, A RISK OF DAMNUM ABSQUE INJURIA.
FINALLY.. LEGES POSTERIORES PRIORES CONTRARIAS ABROGANT.
I TRUST I MAKE MYSELF COMPLETELY CLEAR.
POMPOSITY IS NEXT TO GODLINESS
CLICK!

THERE SITS SIR GEOFFREY BENTWOOD QC, FINEST LEGAL MIND OF HIS GENERATION.
I WONDER WHAT GORDIAN KNOT OF LAW HE IS UNRAVELLING?
INTERESTING DILEMMA... FINELY BALANCED
...ARGUMENTS ON BOTH SIDES...
JAM ROLY-POLY OR CUSTARD TART FOR PUDDING?
INNER TEMPLE LUNCH MENU

A GUIDE TO LEGAL DRAFTING

NEVER CHOOSE SIMPLE WORDS WHERE COMPLEX ONES WILL ~~DO~~ PROVE REASONABLY PRACTICABLE

NEVER USE ONE DOUBLE NEGATIVE WHERE NO TRIPLE NEGATIVE WILL NOT PROVE UNECESSARY.

MAKE FREE USE OF (a) SUB-PARAGRAPHS, and (b) (i) SUB-SUB-PARAGRAPHS and (ii) SCHEDULES

(SEE ATTACHED SCHEDULE)

THE ONLY DOCUMENT YOUR CLIENT SHOULD BE ABLE TO UNDERSTAND IS YOUR BILL.

BUT SIR GEOFFREY, HOW CAN YOU DEFEND SOMEONE YOU KNOW TO BE GUILTY?

WELL, EVERYONE IS ENTITLED TO A PROPER DEFENCE.

THIS IS THE "GOLDEN THREAD" THAT RUNS THROUGH OUR SYSTEM OF JUSTICE.

BUT WHAT IF THEY ESCAPE PUNISHMENT?

AH... THAT THEY DO NOT.

YOU SEE MY DEAR...

...MY FEES ARE ENORMOUS.

... AND ARE PUNISHMENT ENOUGH FOR ANYONE.

'MORNING SIR GEOFFREY, I'VE GOT A NEW SET OF INSTRUCTIONS FOR YOU.

INDEED?

YOU'VE BEEN ASKED TO REPRESENT THE LONDON UNION OF LAP DANCERS IN AN ACTION AGAINST THEIR EMPLOYERS.

THEY NEED YOU TO VISIT ALL THEIR CLUBS AND COMPILE A REPORT ON THEIR WORKING CONDITIONS.

REALLY?

NO.

APRIL FOOL!

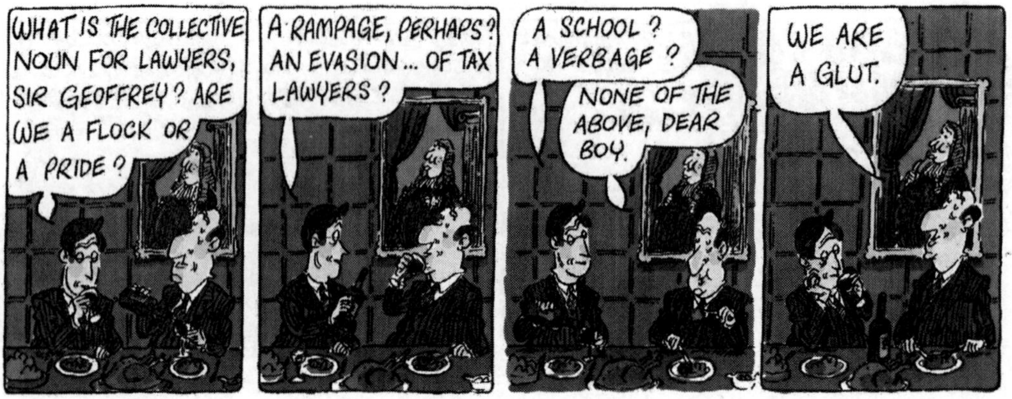
WHAT IS THE COLLECTIVE NOUN FOR LAWYERS, SIR GEOFFREY? ARE WE A FLOCK OR A PRIDE?
A RAMPAGE, PERHAPS? AN EVASION... OF TAX LAWYERS?
A SCHOOL? A VERBAGE?
NONE OF THE ABOVE, DEAR BOY.
WE ARE A GLUT.

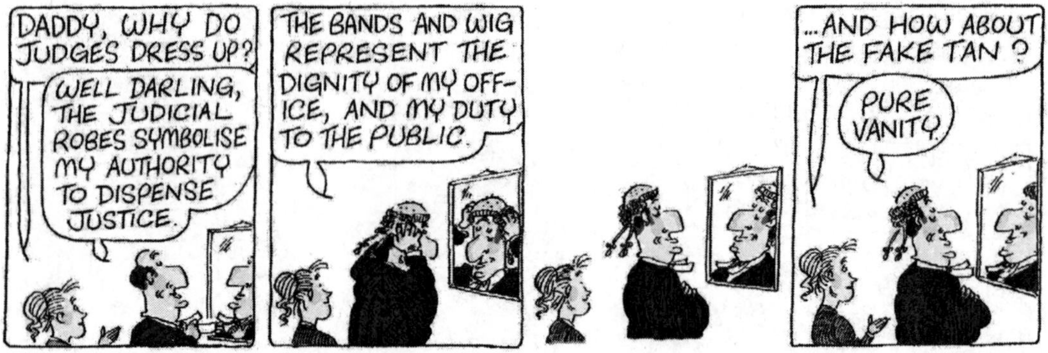
DADDY, WHY DO JUDGES DRESS UP?
WELL DARLING, THE JUDICIAL ROBES SYMBOLISE MY AUTHORITY TO DISPENSE JUSTICE.
THE BANDS AND WIG REPRESENT THE DIGNITY OF MY OFFICE, AND MY DUTY TO THE PUBLIC.
...AND HOW ABOUT THE FAKE TAN?
PURE VANITY.

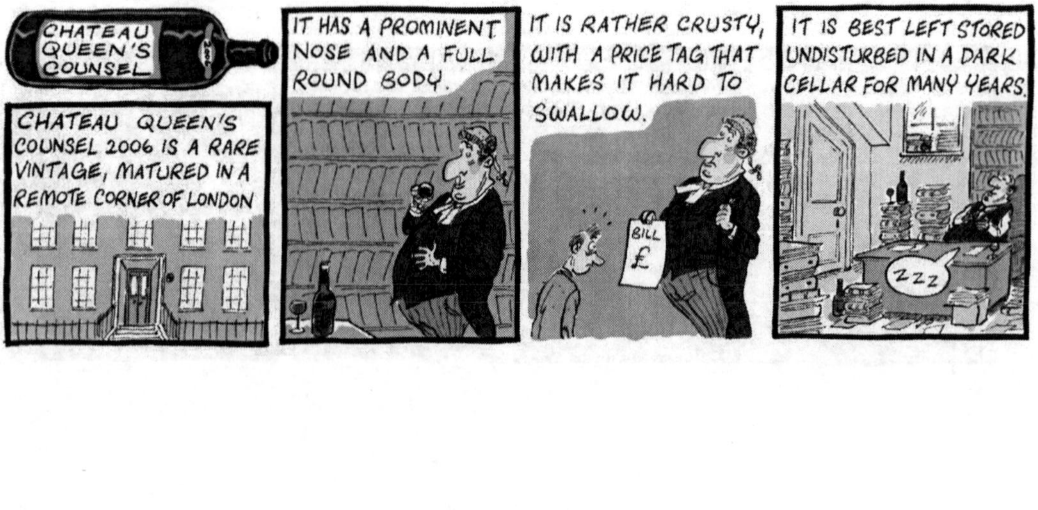
CHATEAU QUEEN'S COUNSEL
CHATEAU QUEEN'S COUNSEL 2006 IS A RARE VINTAGE, MATURED IN A REMOTE CORNER OF LONDON
IT HAS A PROMINENT NOSE AND A FULL ROUND BODY.
IT IS RATHER CRUSTY, WITH A PRICE TAG THAT MAKES IT HARD TO SWALLOW.
BILL £
IT IS BEST LEFT STORED UNDISTURBED IN A DARK CELLAR FOR MANY YEARS.
ZZZ

YES... £250 A MONTH ON WIG MAINTENANCE... AND £400 ON GOWN DRY-CLEANING...
GOSH... I HAD NO IDEA LIFE AS A BARRISTER COULD BE SO EXPENSIVE!
SILVER BUTTONS: £300...
WELL, AT THIS TIME OF YEAR IT IS...
...£550...
SIR GEOFFREY IS DOING HIS TAX RETURN...
GOLD BRAID, £350, VINTAGE CLARET FOR CLIENTS, £1,750...

M'LUD, I MUST STRENUOUSLY OBJECT TO THIS SORT OF BEHAVIOUR.
IT IS OUTRAGEOUS, INSULTING, AND AN ABUSE OF PROTOCOL.
NEVER IN ALL MY YEARS AT THE BAR HAVE I SEEN THE LIKES OF...OF...
... A SOLICITOR, WEARING A WIG, IN OPEN COURT!
BUT SIR GEOFFREY, IT IS PERMITTED BY THE NEW PRACTICE DIRECTION

SO... HOW SHALL WE STAY IN TOUCH? EMAIL?
EMAIL? CERTAINLY NOT... I'VE NO TIME FOR THAT.
BY PHONE THEN?
GOOD HEAVENS NO! I MUST NOT BE DISTURBED.
ER... TEXT MESSAGE?
I INSIST ON PEACE AND QUIET AT ALL TIMES.
WHY THE HELL DOESN'T ANYONE EVER KEEP ME UPDATED ON THE PROGRESS OF THIS CASE?

I'M SORRY RICHARD, BUT THIS IS ONE OF THE WEAKEST CASES I HAVE EVER COME ACROSS.
REALLY? HOW DISAPPOINTING.
I WAS GOING TO INSTRUCT YOU AS LEADER IN THE HIGH COURT AND THE COURT OF APPEAL. NOW I'LL HAVE TO GET SOME-ONE ELSE.
ON REFLECTION, IT DOES APPEAR TO HAVE SOME HIDDEN MERITS...

I'M VERY SORRY, BUT SIR GEOFFREY IS AWAY ON IMPORTANT BUSINESS TODAY
CLERK'S ROOM
I KNOW HE BOOKED A CONFERENCE, BUT SOMETHING CAME UP URGENTLY.
WELL, HIS DIARY SAYS HE HAS A MR JOLLY AT 2PM AND A LADY CLIENT AFTER THAT.
... AND MR JOLLY WINS BY A SHORT HEAD, WITH LADY CLIENT IN SECOND...

DADDY, WHAT'S THE DIFFERENCE BET-WEEN BARRISTERS AND SOLICITORS?
WELL DARLING, THE BAR IS A UNIQUE INSTIT-UTION.
...AN ÉLITE ADVOCACY UNIT AND EXPERT REFERRAL SERVICE.
...COMPOSED OF FEARLESSLY INDEPENDENT PROFESSIONAL INDIVIDUALS!
...BUT MOST OF ALL...
WE GET TO WEAR WIGS AND THEY DON'T.

THE FINANCIAL CRISIS DEEPENED TODAY AS SHAREHOLDERS SEEK COMPENSATION FROM FAILED BANKS...
EXPERTS SUGGEST THAT PENSION FUNDS WILL BRING HUGE CLAIMS FOR THEIR LOSSES...
... LEADING TO EXPENSIVE AND PROTRACTED LITIGATION COSTING MILLIONS OF POUNDS...
MORE BAD NEWS ON THE WIRELESS?
WHAT BAD NEWS?

WHAT DO YOU MAKE OF THE NEW JACKSON REFORMS?
EH?
YOU KNOW, THE NEW RULES ON DBAs
... CHANGES TO CFAs, CPRs AND QOCs
... AND CMCs
SO WHAT DO YOU THINK?
WTF!

DON'T YOU THINK ALL THIS DRESSING UP IS A BIT SILLY? GROWN MEN IN GOWNS, BANDS AND WIGS?
NOT AT ALL.
IT SUITS THE CEREMONY OF THE OCCASION... ALL PART OF AN ANCIENT TRADITION.
WELL... I THINK WE LOOK RIDICULOUS.
NONSENSE CRISPIN, YOU LOOK VERY DIGNIFIED. WELL, WE SHOULD GO IN SOON.
READY, BOYS?
AH... THERE WE ARE...
I'D STILL RATHER GO AS A VICAR.

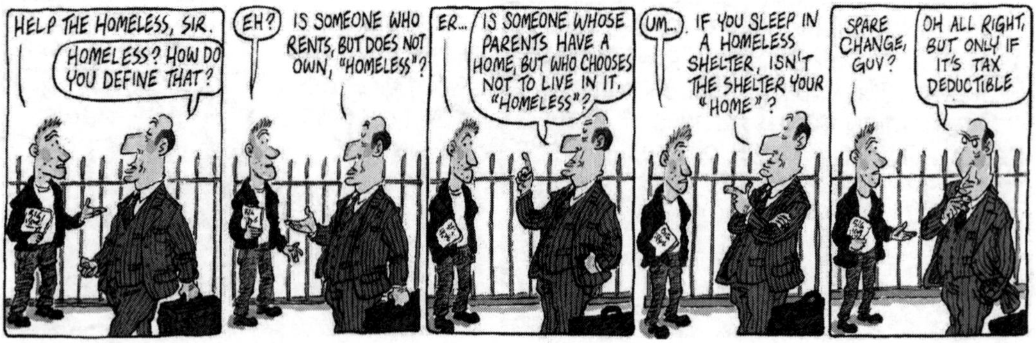
HELP THE HOMELESS, SIR.
HOMELESS? HOW DO YOU DEFINE THAT?
EH?
IS SOMEONE WHO RENTS, BUT DOES NOT OWN, "HOMELESS"?
ER...
IS SOMEONE WHOSE PARENTS HAVE A HOME, BUT WHO CHOOSES NOT TO LIVE IN IT, "HOMELESS"?
UM...
IF YOU SLEEP IN A HOMELESS SHELTER, ISN'T THE SHELTER YOUR "HOME"?
SPARE CHANGE, GUV?
OH ALL RIGHT, BUT ONLY IF IT'S TAX DEDUCTIBLE

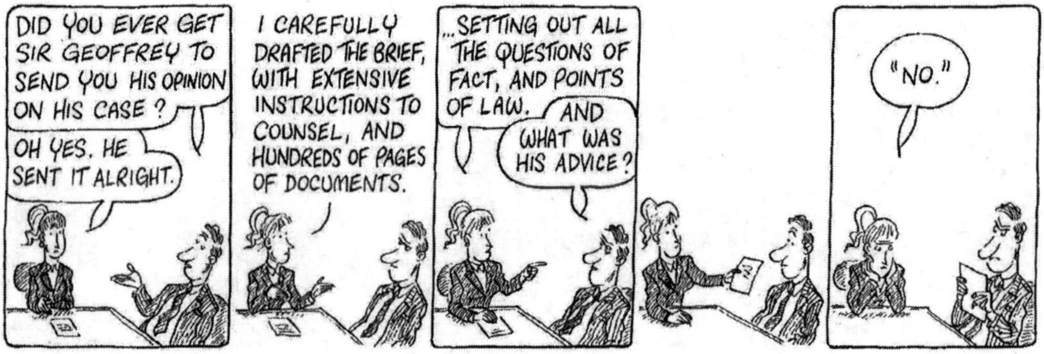
DID YOU EVER GET SIR GEOFFREY TO SEND YOU HIS OPINION ON HIS CASE?
OH YES. HE SENT IT ALRIGHT.
I CAREFULLY DRAFTED THE BRIEF, WITH EXTENSIVE INSTRUCTIONS TO COUNSEL, AND HUNDREDS OF PAGES OF DOCUMENTS.
...SETTING OUT ALL THE QUESTIONS OF FACT, AND POINTS OF LAW.
AND WHAT WAS HIS ADVICE?
"NO."

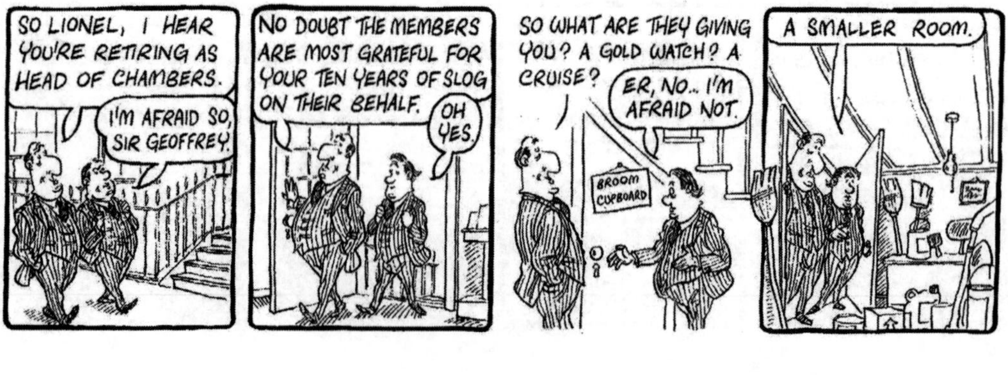
SO LIONEL, I HEAR YOU'RE RETIRING AS HEAD OF CHAMBERS.
I'M AFRAID SO, SIR GEOFFREY.
NO DOUBT THE MEMBERS ARE MOST GRATEFUL FOR YOUR TEN YEARS OF SLOG ON THEIR BEHALF.
OH YES.
SO WHAT ARE THEY GIVING YOU? A GOLD WATCH? A CRUISE?
ER, NO... I'M AFRAID NOT.
BROOM CUPBOARD
A SMALLER ROOM.

I'M AFRAID THAT 2009 WASN'T A GOOD YEAR. CHAMBERS' FINANCES ARE IN POOR SHAPE.
WHAT CAN WE DO TO IMPROVE THINGS ?
WELL, I DO HAVE AN IDEA ...
...BUT I HOPE THE BAR COUNCIL DON'T FIND OUT...
CHAMBERS' 2010 NUDE CALENDAR
2010

HOW'S OUR NEW CHAMBERS' WEBSITE COMING ALONG?
EXCELLENT. LOTS OF NICE GRAPHICS AND PRACTITIONER PROFILES
HAS IT ACTUALLY BROUGHT IN ANY BUSINESS YET ?
WELL...ER...NO. NOT AS SUCH.
BUT WE ARE EXPLORING SOME EXCITING NEW REVENUE STREAMS...
SUCH AS?
WELL... SELLING POP-UP LINKS TO ADULT WEB SITES...

EXCUSE ME YOUNG LADY, BUT JUST WHAT DO YOU THINK YOU'RE WEARING ?
WHAT?
...A TROUSER SUIT, SIR GEOFFREY-WHAT ELSE?
WELL IT WON'T DO!
WE'RE NOT SOME SORT OF TRENDY "HUMAN RIGHTS" CHAMBERS, YOU KNOW. WE MAY BE OLD-FASHIONED, BUT WE HAVE STANDARDS!
... AND I WEAR THE TROUSERS AROUND HERE.

DID YOU CELEBRATE THE DIAMOND JUBILEE?
CERTAINLY NOT!
I AM A REPUBLICAN!
NO-ONE SHOULD RULE FOR AN INDEFINITE PERIOD!
SPEAKING OF WHICH...
ISN'T IT TIME YOU STEPPED DOWN AS HEAD OF CHAMBERS?
THAT IS COMPLETELY DIFFERENT!
... ANYWAY MY NEPHEW, GEOFFREY JUNIOR, WILL SOON SUCCEED ME.

I SEE THE GOVERNMENT WANTS TO DROP THE "CROWN" FROM "CROWN PROSECUTION SERVICE."
QUITE RIGHT. THE LEGAL SYSTEM MUST MOVE WITH THE TIMES.
YES... I SUPPOSE THEY'LL DROP THE "QUEEN" FROM "QUEEN'S COUNSEL" NEXT.
HAVE THESE PEOPLE NO RESPECT FOR TRADITION? THAT'S A TERRIBLE IDEA!

GEOFFREY BENTWOOD, 4 LAWN BUILDINGS...
HELLO, I REPRESENT THE JUDICIAL SELECTION DIVISION OF THE LORD CHANCELLOR'S DEPARTMENT...
WE'D LIKE TO OFFER YOU A HIGH COURT JUDGE-SHIP...
I... I... WELL I HARDLY...
PLUS, OF COURSE, A DRIVER, SECRETARY, AND PERSONAL BODYGUARD...
YES... WELL, I...
... AND PERSONAL MASSEUSE AND... HA! HA! HA!
ER...?
APRIL FOOL!
CLICK!

SIR GEOFFREY, JUDGEMENT IN YOUR CASE HAS ARRIVED.
LET'S HEAR IT THEN.
KNOCK! KNOCK!
ER... "AT THE OUTSET, LET ME THANK SIR GEOFFREY FOR HIS HELPFUL AND SUCCINCT SUBMISSIONS...
"IT IS DIFFICULT TO THINK OF A POINT IN HIS CLIENT'S FAVOUR THAT HE MISSED..."
STOP, I'VE HEARD ENOUGH
WHEN THE JUDGE COMPLEMENTS YOUR ARGUMENT...
YOU KNOW YOU'VE LOST
I'M AFRAID SO.

LADIES AND GENTLEMEN, LEGAL REFORM HAS DONE LITTLE TO CUT THE COST OF LITIGATION. MOST CASES STILL GO ON FAR TOO LONG.
BARRISTER'S SPEECHES MUST BE SHORTENED. THERE MUST BE TIME LIMITS.
REMEMBER THAT THE SOUL OF GOOD ADVOCACY IS BREVITY.
... AND FINALLY, TO RECAP POINTS 11-123 OF MY SPEECH...
ZZ
ZZZ

COMING TO CHAMBERS' JUBILEE PARTY?
I DON'T KNOW...
OH GO ON...
SIXTY YEARS OF RULE... A LONG AND GLORIOUS REIGN!
OVER HALF A CENTURY OF DEDICATED SERVICE!
...ALRIGHT THEN...
TO SIR GEOFFREY - HEAD OF CHAMBERS FOR AS LONG AS ANYONE CAN REMEMBER!
... AND NEVER ONCE FACED AN ELECTION!

WHERE'S SIR GEOFFREY TODAY?
OH, HE'S SPEAKING AT A RALLY IN SUPPORT OF STRIKING CRIMINAL DEFENCE BARRISTERS.
REALLY?
YES. SOMETHING ABOUT RATES OF PAY FOR LEGAL AID WORK BEING FROZEN.
APPARENTLY THESE STRIKERS ARE QUITE A MILITANT LOT.
WHAT IS IT THAT WE REQUIRE?
MORE MONETARY CONSIDERATION!
WHEN DO WE REQUIRE IT?
PRESENTLY!
EX-WIFE & HOUSE IN COUNTRY TO SUPPORT
KEEP MY KIDS IN PUBLIC SCHOOL

NATURALLY I'LL BE SEEKING IMMEDIATE INTERLOCUTORY RELIEF.
FULL DISCLOSURE OF ASSETS ...MASTER IN CHAMBERS ... COSTS ON THE STANDARD SCALE? GOOD.
CLICK!
TELEPHONE
INTER-LOCUTORY RELIEF
MASTER IN CHAMBERS
DISCLOSE YOUR ASSETS
XXX
CALL ME

MEMBERS OF THE BAR, ALTERNATIVE DISPUTE RESOLUTION, OR "ADR", IS HERE TO STAY.
2002 BAR CONFERENCE
A SIMPLE TORTS CLAIM MIGHT TAKE FIVE YEARS AND FIFTY THOUSAND POUNDS TO COME TO TRIAL.
ADR PROMISES A QUICK, SIMPLE, EFFICIENT, AND LAWYER-FREE PATH TO JUSTICE.
...WHICH IS WHY WE MUST LEARN TO RECOGNISE IT
... AND SQUASH IT LIKE A BUG.

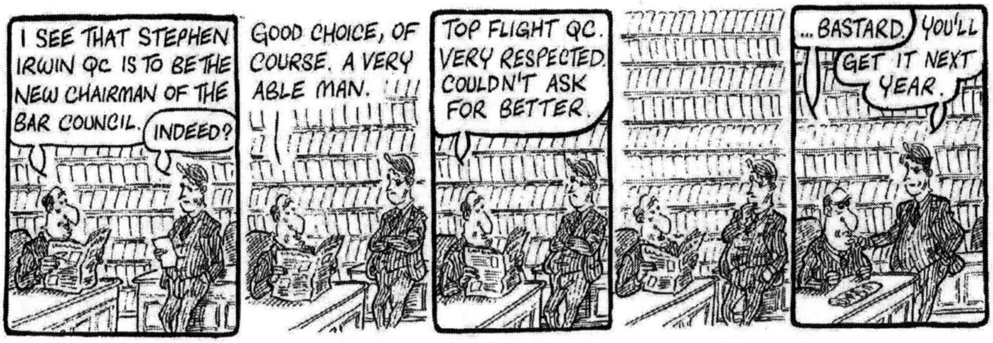
I SEE THAT STEPHEN IRWIN QC IS TO BE THE NEW CHAIRMAN OF THE BAR COUNCIL.
INDEED?
GOOD CHOICE, OF COURSE. A VERY ABLE MAN.
TOP FLIGHT QC. VERY RESPECTED. COULDN'T ASK FOR BETTER.
...BASTARD.
YOU'LL GET IT NEXT YEAR.

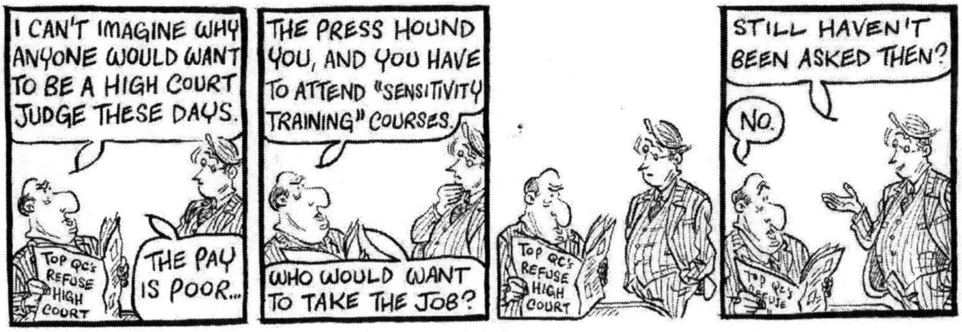
I CAN'T IMAGINE WHY ANYONE WOULD WANT TO BE A HIGH COURT JUDGE THESE DAYS.
TOP QC'S REFUSE HIGH COURT
THE PAY IS POOR...
THE PRESS HOUND YOU, AND YOU HAVE TO ATTEND "SENSITIVITY TRAINING" COURSES.
WHO WOULD WANT TO TAKE THE JOB?
TOP QC'S REFUSE HIGH COURT
STILL HAVEN'T BEEN ASKED THEN?
NO.

CHAPTER FIVE
LAW FIRM ASSOCIATES

Come in on Sunday for our next work-life balance seminar

ACCORDING TO YOUR PERFORMANCE REVIEW, YOU ARE ARGUMENTATIVE, HOSTILE AND UNREASONABLE.
IN ADDITION, IT SEEMS YOU ARE UNCO-OPERATIVE, AND PRONE TO TEMPER TANTRUMS.
IN THE CIRCUMSTANCES, WE HAVE ONLY ONE OPTION.
WE'RE TRANSFERRING YOU TO THE LITIGATION DEPARTMENT.
PLIK PLIK

I'M SURPRISED TO LEARN THAT OUR FIRM'S ASSOCIATES ARE BETTER PAID THAN YOURS, RICHARD.
WELL IT JUST GOES TO SHOW, DOESN'T IT?
SHOW WHAT?
...THAT MONEY ISN'T EVERYTHING. BESIDES, MOST OF OUR ASSOCIATES WILL TELL YOU THEY ARE PAID THE GOING RATE.
AND HOW MUCH IS THE GOING RATE?
USUALLY THE LEAST WE CAN GET AWAY WITH WITHOUT THEM GOING.

SO, DID YOU TELL RICHARD YOU WANT TO LEAVE THE FIRM?
YES... HE SAID I COULDN'T GO!
APPARENTLY I'M "PART OF THE FURNITURE" AROUND HERE.
THAT'S NICE.
SORT OF LIKE THE EXPENSIVE CHIPPENDALE CHAIRS IN THE CONFERENCE ROOM?
NO
... MORE LIKE THE PUNCH BAG IN THE GYM.

SECRETS of LEGAL RESEARCH
CAN'T FIND ANYTHING IN THE LAW REPORTS...
...NOTHING IN THE LAW LIBRARY...
...NOTHING IN THE KEY TEXT BOOKS...
...NOTHING ON LEXUS NEXUS...
THERE'S ONLY ONE THING FOR IT.
... WIKIPEDIA.

THIS FIRM EXPECTS INDEPENDENT THOUGHT FROM ITS ASSOCIATES. YOU MUST NEVER FEAR TO DISAGREE OR SPEAK YOUR MIND.
ONE THING THE FIRM WILL NEVER TOLERATE IS YES-MEN.
DO I MAKE MYSELF CLEAR?
YES, MR LOOPHOLE.
GOOD.

the ANNUAL APPRAISAL
YOUR WORK THIS PAST YEAR HAS BEEN EXCELLENT, AND THE FIRM FEELS YOU HAVE A BRIGHT FUTURE.
HOWEVER, TOUGH MARKET CONDITIONS MEAN WE CAN'T OFFER YOU A PARTNERSHIP THIS YEAR.
...OR A BONUS.
...OR A PAY RISE.
...BUT THERE IS ONE IMPORTANT WAY IN WHICH WE CAN SHOW OUR GRATITUDE.
... PLEASE ACCEPT THIS BLUE ENAMEL MERIT BADGE WITH OUR CONGRATULATIONS

THIS YEAR THE FIRM HAS SIGNIFICANTLY REVISED OUR ASSOCIATE BONUS SCHEME.
IN THE CURRENT ECONOMIC CLIMATE WE NEED TO INCENTIVISE OUR STAFF.
THE SUM I HAVE IN MIND FOR YOU IS £10,000.
... WHICH YOU PAY US IF YOU WANT TO KEEP YOUR JOB.
CASH OR CREDIT CARD?

REVENUES ARE DOWN, EXPENSES ARE UP. CAN'T WE GET OUR ASSOCIATES TO WORK HARDER?
BUT THEY WORK INSANE HOURS AS IT IS.
ONE PASSED OUT AT HIS DESK FROM OVERWORK ONLY LAST WEEK!
WELL, LET'S FIRE SOME THEN IF THEY CAN'T TAKE THE PACE!
NO... ALL THAT WOULD DO IS DECREASE OUR BILLINGS...
WELL THERE MUST BE SOME WAY WE CAN SQUEEZE MORE WORK OUT OF THEM.
LIKE HOW?
WHISPER
GREAT IDEA! LET'S DO IT!
ALRIGHT CRAWLEY, YOU'VE HAD YOUR THREE MINUTES — TIME'S UP
TIME IS MONEY
I'LL BE RIGHT WITH YOU!

NO BONUS AGAIN THIS YEAR, AND SALARIES FROZEN.
MORE REDUNDANCIES, AND BENEFITS CUT BACK.
RACHEL, WE NEED YOU TO COME IN THIS WEEKEND.
WHY?
"EMPLOYEE CAREER DEVELOPMENT COURSE", SUNDAY AT 9am.

FINALLY, THE END OF THE DAY... NO MORE LAW !
WAP!
NO MORE GORDIAN KNOTS OF LEGAL PROBLEMS TO UNTANGLE.
TIME TO PARTY!
SO YOU'RE A LAWYER? CAN YOU HELP ME WITH MY MOTHER'S WILL?
MIND IF I BOTHER YOU ABOUT A GARDEN FENCE?
I GOT A SPEEDING TICKET. HOW CAN I GET OFF?

MY HUGE CASE IS FINALLY COMING TO AN END... NO MORE INSANE HOURS AT THE OFFICE.
I'VE FINALLY GOT MY LIFE BACK, AND CAN RELAX AND BREATHE AGAIN...
www.qccartoon.com
... LIFE CAN GO BACK TO NORMAL...
i.e. WORRYING ABOUT KEEPING MY JOB...
RACHEL, YOUR BILLINGS ARE WAY DOWN
PULL YOUR FINGER OUT!

AH RACHEL, I'LL NEED A FEW DAYS WORK FROM YOU ON THIS FILE.
SORRY...
...NO TIME !
GREAT- I'LL TELL THE CLIENT TO EXPECT IT NEXT WEEK.
NO, REALLY...
...I'M SWAMPED!
HI MATT, I'VE GOT RACHEL HERE; SHE SAYS SHE'LL HAVE IT BY MONDAY.
BUT... BUT...
OH AND BY THE WAY YOU MUSTN'T LET THE OTHER PARTNERS BULLY YOU INTO TAKING ON EXTRA WORK.
YOU MUST FIGHT YOUR CORNER!

BACK TO WORK, BACK TO A HUGE HEAP OF FILES AND DEADLINES.
HOW AM I EVER GOING TO GET ALL THIS DONE?
THERE'S ONLY ONE THING FOR IT...
...DISTRACT MYSELF BY SPENDING THE DAY SURFING THE WEB FOR CELEBRITY GOSSIP.
TAP TAP

IT'S SO UNFAIR THAT ASSOCIATES GET EXCLUDED FROM PARTNERSHIP MEETINGS.
ALL THE IMPORTANT ISSUES AFFECTING THE FIRM... AND WE HAVE NO SAY AT ALL!
ONE DAY WE'LL BE THERE, MAKING THE BIG DECISIONS!
SO WE'RE AGREED THEN... ALL FUTURE DECISIONS ON COFFEE ROOM SUPPLIES WILL BE HANDLED BY THE BISCUIT SUB-COMMITTEE...

ER... RICHARD... I'D LIKE TO TAKE A WEEK OFF THIS SUMMER IF THAT'S OK...
OF COURSE, RACHEL! I CAN'T REMEMBER WHEN YOU LAST HAD A HOLIDAY!
THANKYOU! THAT'S GREAT! THAT'S...
NATURALLY YOU'LL HAVE TO GIVE AN UNDERTAKING THAT NO WORK WILL NEED TO BE DONE ON ANY OF YOUR CASES WHILE YOU'RE AWAY.
BUT I... I CAN'T POSSIBLY... ...I MEAN, CAN'T SOMEONE ELSE... ?
...I SUPPOSE I'LL HAVE TO STAY THEN.
WHAT A TROOPER!
–YOU WON'T MIND LOOKING AFTER A FEW OF MY FILES WHILE I'M IN TUSCANY THEN.

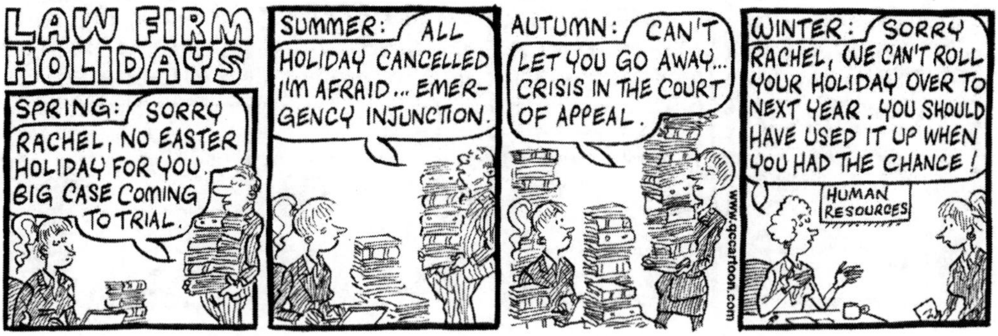
LAW FIRM HOLIDAYS
SPRING: SORRY RACHEL, NO EASTER HOLIDAY FOR YOU. BIG CASE COMING TO TRIAL.
SUMMER: ALL HOLIDAY CANCELLED I'M AFRAID... EMERGENCY INJUNCTION.
AUTUMN: CAN'T LET YOU GO AWAY... CRISIS IN THE COURT OF APPEAL.
www.qccartoon.com
WINTER: SORRY RACHEL, WE CAN'T ROLL YOUR HOLIDAY OVER TO NEXT YEAR. YOU SHOULD HAVE USED IT UP WHEN YOU HAD THE CHANCE!
HUMAN RESOURCES

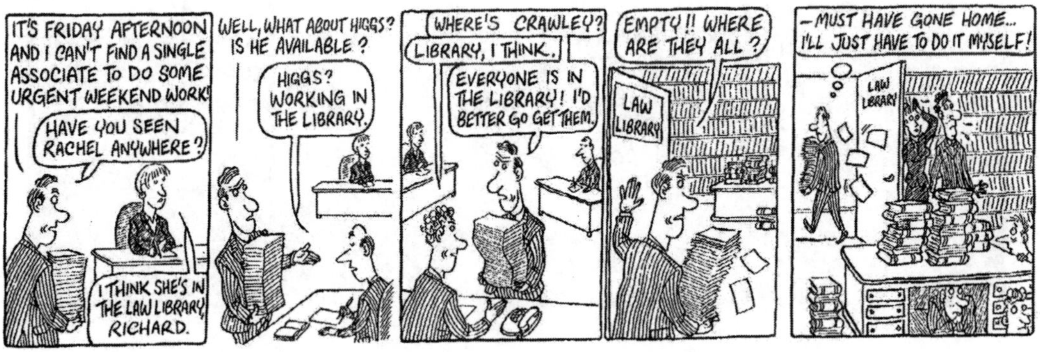
IT'S FRIDAY AFTERNOON AND I CAN'T FIND A SINGLE ASSOCIATE TO DO SOME URGENT WEEKEND WORK!
HAVE YOU SEEN RACHEL ANYWHERE?
I THINK SHE'S IN THE LAW LIBRARY, RICHARD.
WELL, WHAT ABOUT HIGGS? IS HE AVAILABLE?
HIGGS? WORKING IN THE LIBRARY.
WHERE'S CRAWLEY?
LIBRARY, I THINK.
EVERYONE IS IN THE LIBRARY! I'D BETTER GO GET THEM.
EMPTY!! WHERE ARE THEY ALL?
LAW LIBRARY
– MUST HAVE GONE HOME... I'LL JUST HAVE TO DO IT MYSELF!
LAW LIBRARY

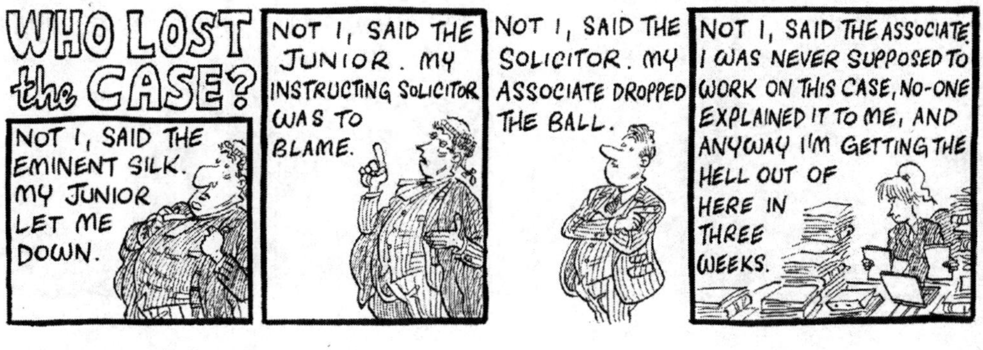
WHO LOST the CASE?
NOT I, SAID THE EMINENT SILK. MY JUNIOR LET ME DOWN.
NOT I, SAID THE JUNIOR. MY INSTRUCTING SOLICITOR WAS TO BLAME.
NOT I, SAID THE SOLICITOR. MY ASSOCIATE DROPPED THE BALL.
NOT I, SAID THE ASSOCIATE. I WAS NEVER SUPPOSED TO WORK ON THIS CASE, NO-ONE EXPLAINED IT TO ME, AND ANYWAY I'M GETTING THE HELL OUT OF HERE IN THREE WEEKS.

I HATE MY JOB. I FANTASISE ABOUT QUITTING ALL THE TIME.
OH?
SOMETIMES I FEEL AS IF I AM A PRISONER OF THE FIRM!
SO WHY NOT LEAVE?
OH, I COULDN'T DO THAT! THEY NEED ME!
I THINK I'VE GOT STOCKHOLM SYNDROME...

RICHARD, I THINK THIS CLAIM IS A BIT OUTSIDE MY FIELD OF EXPERTISE.
REALLY?
WELL... I JUST DON'T FEEL AS IF I ADD ANYTHING TO THE CASE.
OF COURSE YOU DO!
YOU ADD A GREAT DEAL!
YOU ADD TO THE AMOUNT OF TIME WE CAN BILL THE CLIENT.

WHAT DO YOU THINK OF THAT NEW ASSOCIATE?
HIGGS?
ISN'T HE CUTE?
NO WAY! HE'S SHORT, BALDING AND FAT!
HE WEARS GEEKY SPECS AND HARDLY EVER SPEAKS!
YES, BUT...
...YOU SHOULD SEE HIS BILLINGS!

AS YOUR FIRM'S BUSINESS CONSULTANT, I MUST REPORT THAT EXPENSES ARE RISING FASTER THAN REVENUE. YOU NEED TO CUT COSTS.
BUT HOW?
BY GETTING RID OF SOME ASSOCIATES.
SIGH!
AGAIN? SO WE LET THE WEAKEST ONES GO, THEN.
ER... NO... THE STRONGEST.
BUT THAT'S INSANE! WHY?
WELL, IN THE PAST, YOUR STRONGEST ASSOCIATES HAVE LEFT FOR BETTER FIRMS ANYWAY.
...SO MY ADVICE IS TO KEEP THE LEAST COMPETENT, IN THE HOPE THAT THEY MIGHT STICK AROUND.
MAYBE... EVEN MAKE PARTNER SOMEDAY?

RACHEL, I NEED THIS DRAFTED BY TOMORROW. IT'S URGENT.
BUT I'VE GOT A DOZEN "URGENT" ITEMS ON MY DESK!
EVERY PARTNER WHO WALKS IN THE DOOR SAYS THEIR WORK IS URGENT!
I MEAN... WHAT ISN'T URGENT AT THIS FIRM?
...ANY WORK YOU DO FOR ANYONE ELSE, OBVIOUSLY.

ANOTHER ONE OF OUR BEST ASSOCIATES HAS LEFT FOR A RIVAL FIRM. WHAT CAN WE DO TO RETAIN THEM?
PAY THEM MORE?
FAR TOO EXPENSIVE.
LET THEM WORK SHORTER HOURS?
NO... THEY BARELY GET THE WORK DONE AS IT IS.
WAIT... I THINK I HAVE THE ANSWER...
TELL ME!
I PLEDGE ALLEGIANCE TO THE FIRM OF PAYE CASH AND PRAYE...

TWO MORE ASSOCIATES HAVE LEFT US FOR OTHER FIRMS.
WHAT? WHY?
OH...MORE MONEY, BETTER CHANCE OF PARTNERSHIP.
GREEDY TRAITORS! AFTER ALL WE'VE DONE FOR THEM!
I KNOW!
...BUT WHAT CAN WE DO TO STOP MORE ASSOCIATES FROM LEAVING?
...GIVE THEM A PAY RISE?
NO. GIVE THEM A PAY CUT.
THAT'LL SHOW 'EM.

ASSOCIATE TORTURE:
a Partner's Guide
CANCEL ALL HOLIDAYS AT THE LAST MINUTE.
BUT... I'M AT AIRPORT SECURITY!
SO?
HAVE THEM SLEEP OUTSIDE YOUR OFFICE IN CASE YOU NEED THEM "URGENTLY".
I FOUND A TYPO!
ZZ
SEND THEM INTO CLIENT MEETINGS WITH NO PRIOR KNOWLEDGE OF THE CASE.
RACHEL HERE IS OUR EXPERT– SHE'LL EXPLAIN EVERYTHING TO YOU.
HAVE THEM DRAFT THEIR OWN REDUNDANCY NOTICE.
Dear Sir or Madam,
TAP TAP

YOUR QUALIFICATIONS ARE IMPECCABLE, BUT THE COMPETITION AT TOP CITY FIRMS LIKE US HAS BEEN VERY FIERCE THIS YEAR.
...AND I'M AFRAID THE FIRM IS LOOKING FOR SOMEONE WITH A BIT MORE...
...HOW SHALL I PUT IT?
...INDIVIDUALITY.

SOMETIMES I GET SO FED UP WITH BEING A LAWYER. THE LONG HOURS, THE UNGRATEFUL CLIENTS,

THE STRESS, THE ENDLESS WORRY, THE GRUMPY PARTNERS...

...BUT THEN I REMEMBER WHY I WENT INTO LAW IN THE FIRST PLACE...

...TO PAY OFF MY STUDENT LOANS.

LET'S SEE... ONE COPY OF THE LITIGATION DOCUMENTS FOR ME... THREE COPIES FOR FILING...

ONE FOR THE COURT, ONE FOR EACH PARTNER, ONE FOR EACH OF THE PARTIES...

CLIENT COPIES, SERVICE COPIES, FIRM COPIES, COPIES FOR EVERYONE I'VE NEVER HEARD OF...

COPIES FOR AN EMERGENCY, COPIES FOR ARCHIVE, COPIES AND COPIES AND COPIES AND COPIES...

HAVE YOU SEEN RACHEL ANYWHERE? SHE WAS HERE COPYING A FEW HOURS AGO...

HERE AT PAYE, CASH & PRAYE WE BELIEVE WE OFFER A UNIQUE SERVICE TO OUR CLIENTS
LAW GRADUATE RECRUITMENT FAIR

OUR MISSION IS TO BUILD THE WORLD'S No.1 LAW FIRM

WE OFFER UNIQUE OPPORTUNITIES TO GRADUATES SUCH AS YOURSELF, AND ABOVE ALL ...

...WE LIKE TO THINK THAT WE STAND HEAD AND SHOULDERS ABOVE ALL OUR COMPETITORS...

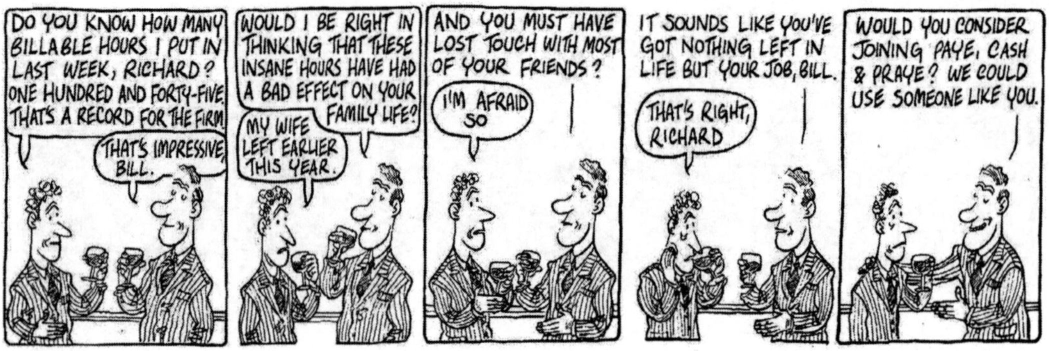
DO YOU KNOW HOW MANY BILLABLE HOURS I PUT IN LAST WEEK, RICHARD? ONE HUNDRED AND FORTY-FIVE. THAT'S A RECORD FOR THE FIRM.
THAT'S IMPRESSIVE, BILL.
WOULD I BE RIGHT IN THINKING THAT THESE INSANE HOURS HAVE HAD A BAD EFFECT ON YOUR FAMILY LIFE?
MY WIFE LEFT EARLIER THIS YEAR.
AND YOU MUST HAVE LOST TOUCH WITH MOST OF YOUR FRIENDS?
I'M AFRAID SO
IT SOUNDS LIKE YOU'VE GOT NOTHING LEFT IN LIFE BUT YOUR JOB, BILL.
THAT'S RIGHT, RICHARD
WOULD YOU CONSIDER JOINING PAYE, CASH & PRAYE? WE COULD USE SOMEONE LIKE YOU.

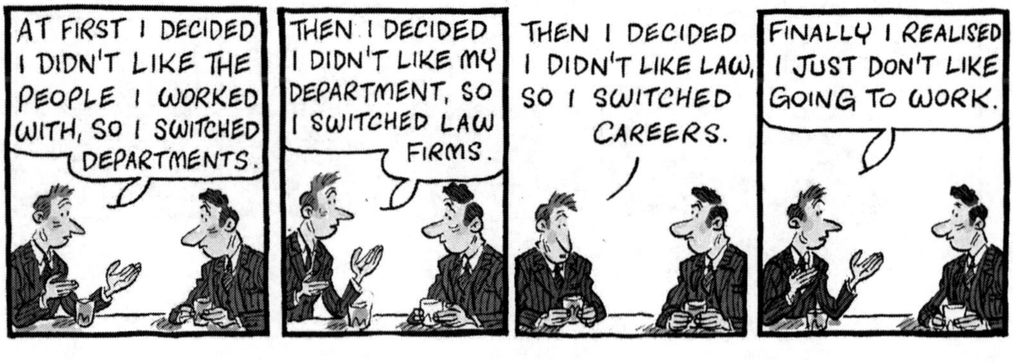
AT FIRST I DECIDED I DIDN'T LIKE THE PEOPLE I WORKED WITH, SO I SWITCHED DEPARTMENTS.
THEN I DECIDED I DIDN'T LIKE MY DEPARTMENT, SO I SWITCHED LAW FIRMS.
THEN I DECIDED I DIDN'T LIKE LAW, SO I SWITCHED CAREERS.
FINALLY I REALISED I JUST DON'T LIKE GOING TO WORK.

CHAPTER SIX
LAW FIRM PARTNERS

Don't think - it weakens the team

HAVE YOU HEARD? THAT CREEP TRAVERS JUST GOT MADE PARTNER!
TRAVERS?! BUT HE'S THICK AS A PLANK! HOW DID HE DO IT?
WELL, HE WAS ALWAYS ONE FOR SUCKING TO THE PARTNERS.
DON'T I KNOW IT! A REAL BOOT-LICKER!
HEY — WATCH OUT! HERE HE COMES!
CREAK!
WELL DONE TRAVERS!
VERY WELL DESERVED.

I'M SORRY, RICHARD, I'VE MADE A BIG MISTAKE.
WHAT'S THAT?
ER... I DRAFTED A CONTRACT FOR OUR BIGGEST CLIENT.
...AND I MESSED UP THE MAIN CLAUSE. THEY'LL PROBABLY BE SUED.
THEY ARE BEING SUED.
OH NO!
YES, BUT DON'T WORRY.
... THEY'VE JUST INSTRUCTED US ON THE LITIGATION.

I'M SORRY, BUT THAT'S NOT AN ACCEPTABLE SETTLEMENT OFFER.
£100,000 IS JUST NOT ENOUGH.
AFTER ALL...
MY CLIENT NEEDS SOMETHING TOO.

BEING A PARTNER AT A HUGE LAW FIRM ISN'T WHAT IT'S CRACKED UP TO BE.
I'VE GOT THE GLUMS. I WONDER WHAT I CAN DO TO CHEER MYSELF UP?
I KNOW... I'LL CALL ONE OF THE ASSOCIATES...
PLIK PLIK
RACHEL- WHAT DID YOU THINK OF THAT CONTRACT I DRAFTED?
OH... IT WAS A WORK OF GENIUS, RICHARD.
I FEEL SO MUCH BETTER NOW...

BANKERS FACE NEW CRITICISM AS THE FINANCIAL CRISIS CONTINUES...
TAP TAP
PUBLIC CONFIDENCE IN POLITICIANS FALLS TO NEW LOWS...
ESTATE AGENTS ARE BLAMED FOR THE DIRE STATE OF THE HOUSING MARKET...
www.gccartoon.com
IT'S SO GOOD TO BE A LAWYER... HARDLY ANYONE HATES US ANYMORE.

NEW COMPUTER, RICHARD?
IT'S A SERIES 3 LITIGATOR 2001.
WHAT CAN IT DO?
EVERYTHING A HUMAN LAWYER CAN DO, ONLY BETTER!
SUCH AS?
OH... OVERBILL...
...FORCE ASSOCIATES TO WORK LATE... ...ABUSE THE SECRETARIAL STAFF...
... BUT THE BEST THING IS...
TAP TAP
... WHATEVER FONT YOU SELECT, IT ALWAYS COMES OUT IN FINE PRINT!
WHIRRR

ITEM ONE ON TODAY'S AGENDA IS THE SUBJECT OF SPONSORSHIP.
I BELIEVE THAT OUR FIRM SHOULD SPONSOR A LOCAL EVENT OR EXHIBITION... SOMETHING THAT TELLS THE WORLD EXACTLY WHO WE ARE.
... YOUNG, DYNAMIC, FLEXIBLE, MODERN AND ADAPTIVE.
SOMETHING'S NOT RIGHT HERE...
SPONSORED BY FILLIBUSTER & LOOPHOLE SOLICITORS

WHY THE LONG FACE RICHARD?
OH... THE FIRM'S ANNUAL NUMBERS ARE JUST IN.
BUT I THOUGHT YOU HAD A RECORD YEAR!
I DID!
SO WHAT'S THE PROBLEM?
BECAUSE...
IT MEANS I'LL HAVE TO DO EVEN BETTER NEXT YEAR

HAVE YOU EVER THOUGHT OF QUITTING THE FIRM, RICHARD?
ONCE, YES. MANY YEARS AGO.
IT WAS AT A TIME WHEN I THOUGHT THE FIRM WAS HEADED FOR BIG TROUBLE.
HOW SO?
OH... BY LETTING IN THE WRONG SORT OF PERSON.
... LOWERING STANDARDS. RIGHT THEN, I KNEW I SHOULD HAVE NO PART IN IT.
WHEN WAS THIS?
... WHEN THEY OFFERED ME A PARTNERSHIP.

I DON'T BELIEVE IT. THIS CHEQUE IS FOR FAR TOO MUCH MONEY. WE'VE BEEN OVERPAID.
WHAT AN ETHICAL DILEMMA. WHAT SHOULD I DO ?
SHOULD I... SHOULD I...
SHOULD I TELL MY PARTNER ?

HOW TO TRANSLATE LEGALESE
HELLO MR SPROCKET, HOW ARE THINGS ?
GOT ANY NEW BUSINESS FOR ME?
...NO... I HAVEN'T HEARD FROM THE OTHER SIDE LATELY.
RATS. FORGOT TO CALL THEM.
GOOD QUESTION... I'LL HAVE TO GET BACK TO YOU ON THAT.
HAVEN'T GOT A CLUE.
SAY HELLO TO YOUR LOVELY WIFE.
WHAT WAS HER NAME AGAIN ?

RACHEL, WE CAN'T SEND THIS INVOICE OUT WITH NO PARTNER TIME ON IT. THE CLIENT WILL REALISE YOU DID ALL THE WORK WITH NO SUPERVISION !
BUT RICHARD...
BILL £
WE CAN'T BILL THE CLIENT FOR TIME YOU DIDN'T SPEND !
HM. I SUPPOSE YOU'RE RIGHT.
WELL SEND IT OUT AS IT IS THEN.
— I'LL DICTATE A COVERING LETTER TO EXPLAIN THE SITUATION.
Dear Mr Sprocket, Please find our invoice enclosed. As one of our most valued clients...
You have not been charged for my time on this transaction.

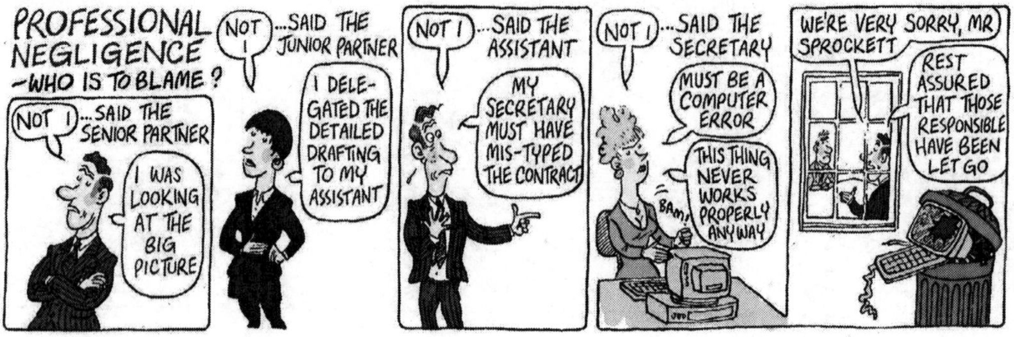
PROFESSIONAL NEGLIGENCE -WHO IS TO BLAME?
NOT I ...SAID THE SENIOR PARTNER
I WAS LOOKING AT THE BIG PICTURE
NOT I ...SAID THE JUNIOR PARTNER
I DELEGATED THE DETAILED DRAFTING TO MY ASSISTANT
NOT I ...SAID THE ASSISTANT
MY SECRETARY MUST HAVE MIS-TYPED THE CONTRACT
NOT I ...SAID THE SECRETARY
MUST BE A COMPUTER ERROR
THIS THING NEVER WORKS PROPERLY ANYWAY
BAM!
WE'RE VERY SORRY, MR SPROCKETT
REST ASSURED THAT THOSE RESPONSIBLE HAVE BEEN LET GO

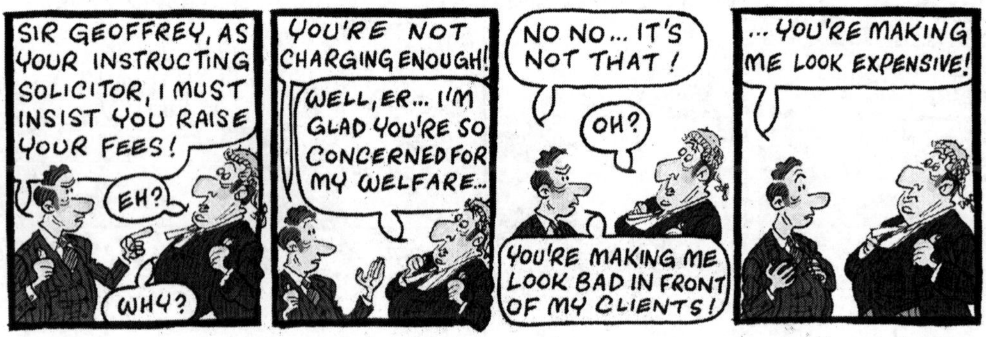
SIR GEOFFREY, AS YOUR INSTRUCTING SOLICITOR, I MUST INSIST YOU RAISE YOUR FEES!
EH?
WHY?
YOU'RE NOT CHARGING ENOUGH!
WELL, ER... I'M GLAD YOU'RE SO CONCERNED FOR MY WELFARE...
NO NO... IT'S NOT THAT!
OH?
YOU'RE MAKING ME LOOK BAD IN FRONT OF MY CLIENTS!
... YOU'RE MAKING ME LOOK EXPENSIVE!

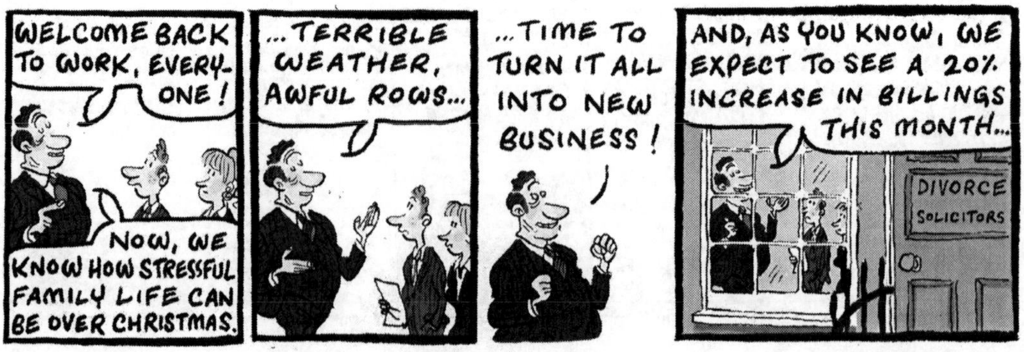
WELCOME BACK TO WORK, EVERYONE!
NOW, WE KNOW HOW STRESSFUL FAMILY LIFE CAN BE OVER CHRISTMAS.
...TERRIBLE WEATHER, AWFUL ROWS...
...TIME TO TURN IT ALL INTO NEW BUSINESS!
AND, AS YOU KNOW, WE EXPECT TO SEE A 20% INCREASE IN BILLINGS THIS MONTH...
DIVORCE SOLICITORS

GENTLEMEN, I THINK WE'RE AGREED THAT WE HAVE TO LET HIM GO.
I KNOW HE'S BEEN A PARTNER FOR DECADES, BUT HE'S JUST NOT BILLING THE HOURS ANYMORE.
WE CAN'T AFFORD TO BE SENTI-MENTAL ABOUT DEAD WOOD HERE AT PAYE, CASH & PRAYE.
SEND HIM IN, PLEASE
PRESS
THANKS FOR COMING IN, DAD. WE NEED TO TALK.

HOW DID THAT BIG CASE OF YOURS GO, RICHARD?
EXCELLENT – WE TRAMPLED ALL OVER THEM!
WE TIED THEM UP IN KNOTS IN DISCOVERY – EXCHANGED OVER A MILLION DOCUMENTS!
...FLOODED THEM WITH INTERROGATORIES AND OVERWHELMED THEM WITH INTERLOCUTORY APPLICATIONS!
SO YOU WON THE CASE?
ACTUALLY, WE LOST
BUT WE DID A GREAT JOB BEATING UP THE OTHER SIDE!

ALL THE LARGE CITY LAW FIRMS ARE WRITING TO THEIR CLIENTS, SEEKING TO EXCLUDE LIABILITY FOR ALL WORK DONE BETWEEN MIDNIGHT AND 6AM.
...AND I THINK IT'S HIGH TIME THAT OUR FIRM DID THE SAME.
BUT RICHARD, WE ALMOST NEVER WORK THAT LATE.
HM... I SUPPOSE YOU'RE RIGHT. WELL... IN THAT CASE...
...LET'S EXCLUDE LIABILITY FOR ALL WORK DONE AFTER LUNCHTIME.
EXCELLENT PLAN.

LAW FiRM TiME SHEETS TRANSLATED
Research - 3½ hrs.
TRANSLATION: SURFING the WEB.
CLICK CLICK
Drafting: 1 hr.
TRANSLATION: EATING LUNCH AT YOUR DESK.
MUNCH
Misc. Legal Forms.
TRANSLATION: ORDERING GIFTS ONLINE.
Preparing for Meeting.
ENGAGED

PARTNERESE TRANSLATED
ER... JUST DASH OFF A QUICK DRAFT OF THIS PROSPECTUS, WOULD YOU?
TRANSLATION: GIVE ME A POLISHED, FINAL DRAFT SUITABLE FOR FRAMING.
...AND JUST SKIM THE CASE AUTHORITY TO MAKE SURE WE'RE COVERED.
TRANSLATION: LOOK UP EVERY CASE OF THE REMOTEST IMPORTANCE.
DON'T SPEND MORE THAN A FEW HOURS ON IT.
TRANSLATION: YOU STILL HAVE TO GET ALL OF YOUR OTHER WORK DONE.
ENJOY YOUR WEEKEND.
TRANSLATION: DON'T EVEN THINK OF NOT HAVING THIS DONE BY MONDAY MORNING.

YOUR APPRAISAL IS EXCELLENT, BUT I'M AFRAID THE FIRM FACES AN EXTREMELY TOUGH ECONOMIC CLIMATE.
BELTS MUST BE TIGHTENED, AND ASSOCIATE BONUSES SACRIFICED.
PAY CUTS MUST BE MADE ACROSS THE BOARD.
... IF THE PARTNERS ARE GOING TO CONTINUE TO TAKE HOME £500,000 A YEAR...

BUSINESS IS TERRIBLE, WE MUST CUT COSTS. HOW ABOUT WE LOSE SOME ASSOCIATES ?
NO...
WE'VE CUT THEM TO THE BONE ALREADY.
WHAT ABOUT H.R.?
NO... THEY'RE ALL FRIENDS WITH THE SENIOR PARTNERS.
MARKETING ?
...SAME PROBLEM.
HOW ABOUT I.T. ? THEY'RE ALL GEEKS AND NO-ONE KNOWS WHAT THEY DO ANYWAY.
GREAT IDEA!
LATER...
HEY... WHY THE HELL DOESN'T MY COMPUTER WORK?
BANG!

I DON'T KNOW... IT JUST SEEMS ODD... A GROUP OF ELDERLY WHITE MEN SELECTING THEIR NEW LEADER IN SECRET.
ROME LATEST
CLOSED DOORS, NO WOMEN, AND EXCOMMUNICATION FOR BREAKING THE SILENCE !
WELL...
ROME
...I SUPPOSE THE PROCESS OF ELECTING A NEW POPE COULD BE MORE OPEN.
NO ... NOT THE POPE !
THE ELECTION OF A NEW SENIOR PARTNER!
KEEP OUT
DO NOT DISTURB

PARTNERSHIP DISTRIBUTION NOT BAD THIS YEAR, EH?
NOT BAD AT ALL
WHAT WILL YOU DO WITH THE WINDFALL?
OH, I DON'T KNOW...
BARBADOS WITH THE KIDS, PERHAPS.
MAYBE A NEW MERCEDES FOR THE WIFE
HERE'S TO A MOST SATISFACTORY END TO THE FINANCIAL YEAR.
I'LL DRINK TO THAT
YOUR ROUND, I THINK?
ER... YOURS
SORRY, NO CASH LEFT
I JUST GOT ONE

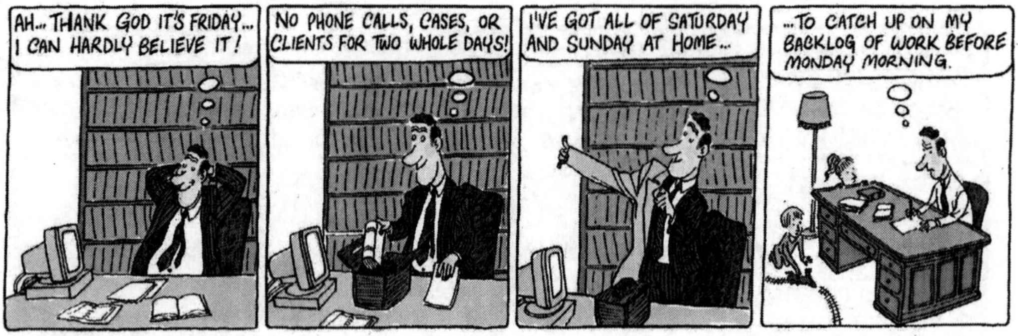
AH... THANK GOD IT'S FRIDAY... I CAN HARDLY BELIEVE IT!
NO PHONE CALLS, CASES, OR CLIENTS FOR TWO WHOLE DAYS!
I'VE GOT ALL OF SATURDAY AND SUNDAY AT HOME...
...TO CATCH UP ON MY BACKLOG OF WORK BEFORE MONDAY MORNING.

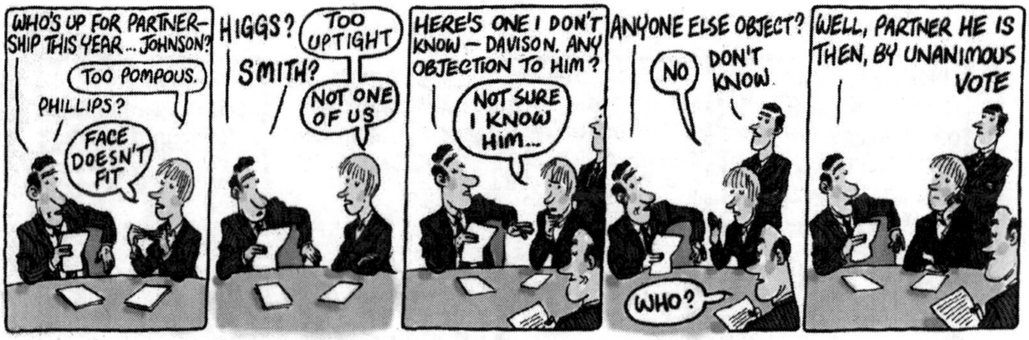
WHO'S UP FOR PARTNERSHIP THIS YEAR... JOHNSON?
TOO POMPOUS.
PHILLIPS?
FACE DOESN'T FIT
HIGGS?
TOO UPTIGHT
SMITH?
NOT ONE OF US
HERE'S ONE I DON'T KNOW – DAVISON. ANY OBJECTION TO HIM?
NOT SURE I KNOW HIM...
ANYONE ELSE OBJECT?
NO
DON'T KNOW
WHO?
WELL, PARTNER HE IS THEN, BY UNANIMOUS VOTE

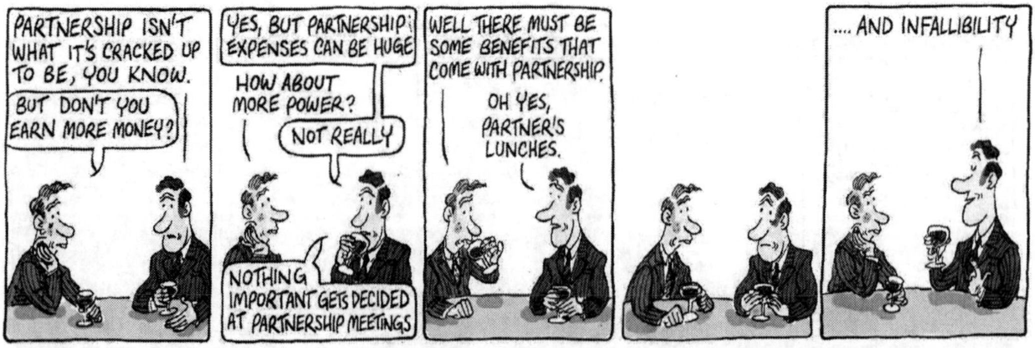
PARTNERSHIP ISN'T WHAT IT'S CRACKED UP TO BE, YOU KNOW.
BUT DON'T YOU EARN MORE MONEY?
YES, BUT PARTNERSHIP EXPENSES CAN BE HUGE
HOW ABOUT MORE POWER?
NOT REALLY
NOTHING IMPORTANT GETS DECIDED AT PARTNERSHIP MEETINGS
WELL THERE MUST BE SOME BENEFITS THAT COME WITH PARTNERSHIP.
OH YES, PARTNER'S LUNCHES.
.... AND INFALLIBILITY

HOW'S LAW TREATING YOU?
OH... I USED TO BE A LAWYER, BUT I GAVE IT UP. NOW I WORK IN SALES.
SALES? BUT I THOUGHT YOU WERE A PARTNER IN A LAW FIRM?
I AM.
THAT'S THE PROBLEM.
...ALL I DO IS PLAY GOLF WITH MY CLIENTS AND TAKE THEM TO LUNCH. I HAVEN'T PRACTISED LAW IN YEARS.

...SO HE SAID "THIS IS A CLEAR CASE OF RES IPSA LOQUITUR" WHEN HE REALLY MEANT "DAMNUM ABSQUE INJURIA".
HA! HA! HA!
HO! HO! HO!
YOU KNOW, FOR SOME REASON I HARDLY KNOW ANYONE WHO ISN'T A LAWYER ANYMORE.
...ME NEITHER.

IT'S PATHETIC WHAT SOME FIRMS WILL DO TO GET INTO THE LOCAL PAPER
I KNOW...
LOOK... BINDER & BRIEF-CASE ARE DOING A SPONSORED BIKE RIDE BACKWARDS DOWN THE HIGH STREET.
MM...
YOU WOULDN'T CATCH THIS FIRM STOOPING SO LOW FOR A BIT OF FREE PUBLICITY.
OH NO
WELL RICHARD, HOW DOES IT FIT?
THE FEATHERS ARE MAKING MY NOSE ITCH

ASSOCIATE TORTURE:
a Partner's Guide
CANCEL ALL HOLIDAYS AT THE LAST MINUTE.
BUT... I'M AT AIRPORT SECURITY!
SO?
HAVE THEM SLEEP OUTSIDE YOUR OFFICE IN CASE YOU NEED THEM "URGENTLY".
I FOUND A TYPO!
ZZ
SEND THEM INTO CLIENT MEETINGS WITH NO PRIOR KNOWLEDGE OF THE CASE.
RACHEL HERE IS OUR EXPERT– SHE'LL EXPLAIN EVERYTHING TO YOU.
HAVE THEM DRAFT THEIR OWN REDUNDANCY NOTICE.
Dear Sir or Madam,
TAP TAP

YOU KNOW, A CASE LIKE THIS SHOULD REALLY BE SETTLED BETWEEN THE PARTIES.
ALL THAT'S LACKING IS A BIT OF GOODWILL ON BOTH SIDES.
A SIMPLE APOLOGY WOULD PROBABLY SOLVE IT.
AGREED.
...WHICH IS WHY OUR CLIENTS MUST NEVER EVER SPEAK.
QUITE RIGHT.

PART OF HAVING "MYSTIQUE" MEANS THAT OUR FIRM NO LONGER OFFERS DISCOUNTS ON OUR FEES.
BUT RICHARD...
I HEARD YOU OFFER A FIFTEEN PERCENT DISCOUNT TO ONE OF OUR BIGGEST CLIENTS!
WELL... MAYBE I DID
BUT IT'S ONLY A DISCOUNT ON MY HOURLY FEE.
I'LL JUST ADD FIFTEEN PERCENT TO MY HOURS.

CHAPTER SEVEN
IN THE COURTS

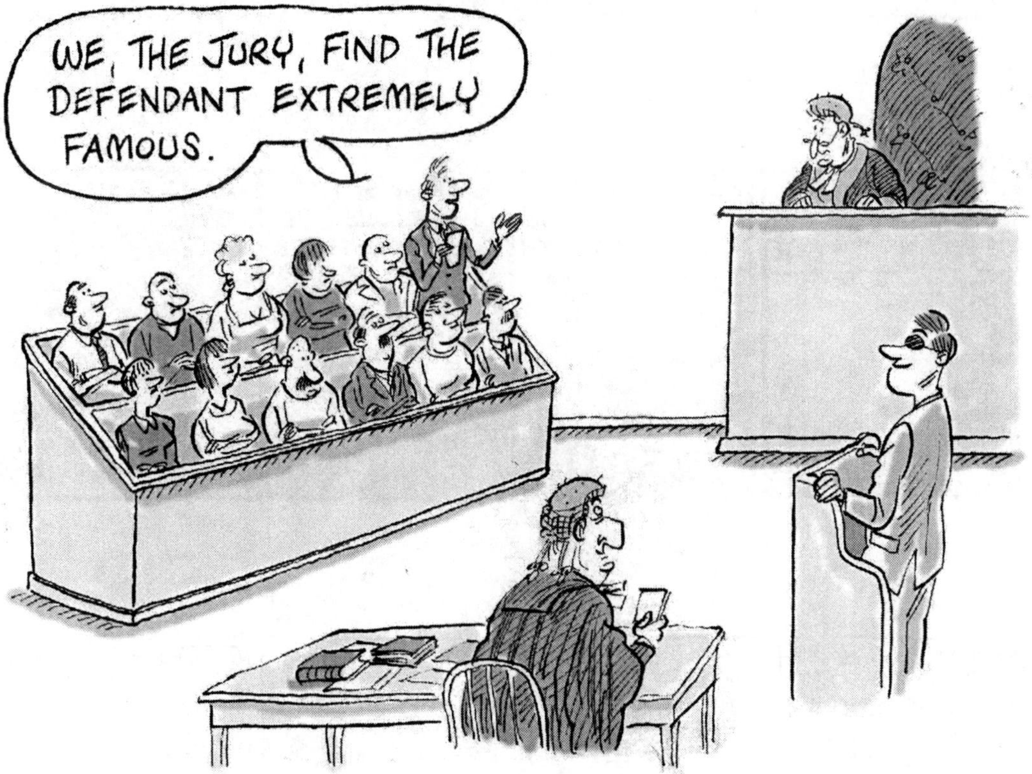
WE, THE JURY, FIND THE DEFENDANT EXTREMELY FAMOUS.

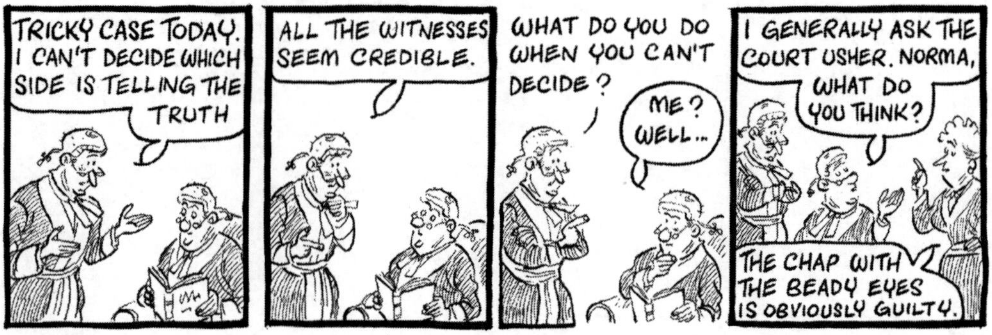
TRICKY CASE TODAY. I CAN'T DECIDE WHICH SIDE IS TELLING THE TRUTH
ALL THE WITNESSES SEEM CREDIBLE.
WHAT DO YOU DO WHEN YOU CAN'T DECIDE?
ME? WELL...
I GENERALLY ASK THE COURT USHER. NORMA, WHAT DO YOU THINK?
THE CHAP WITH THE BEADY EYES IS OBVIOUSLY GUILTY.

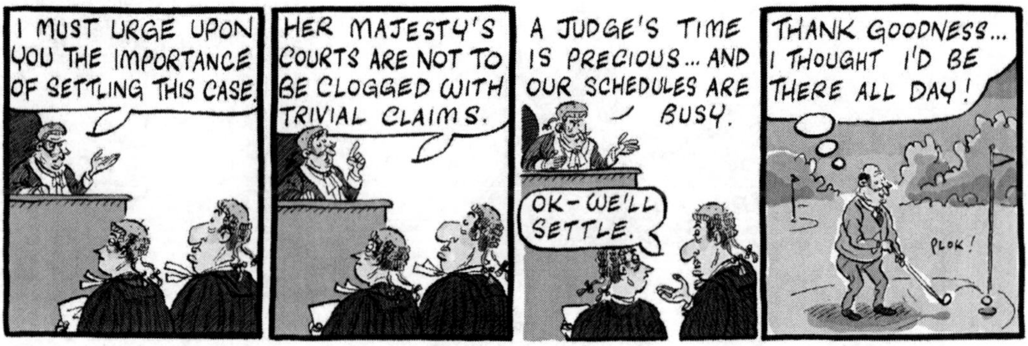
I MUST URGE UPON YOU THE IMPORTANCE OF SETTLING THIS CASE.
HER MAJESTY'S COURTS ARE NOT TO BE CLOGGED WITH TRIVIAL CLAIMS.
A JUDGE'S TIME IS PRECIOUS... AND OUR SCHEDULES ARE BUSY.
OK - WE'LL SETTLE.
THANK GOODNESS... I THOUGHT I'D BE THERE ALL DAY!
PLOK!

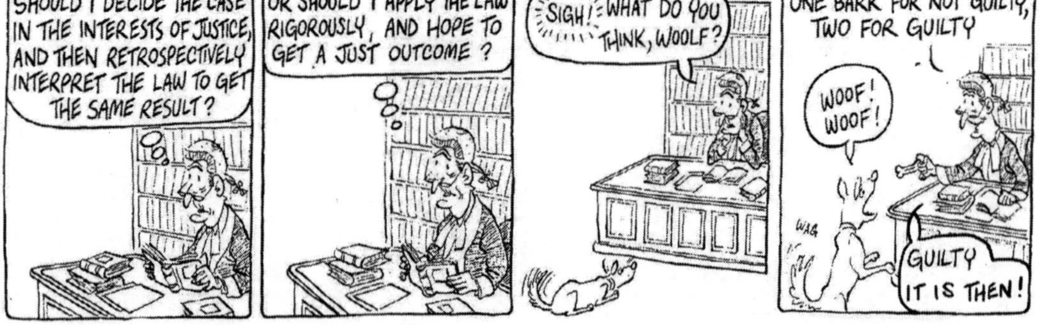
SHOULD I DECIDE THE CASE IN THE INTERESTS OF JUSTICE, AND THEN RETROSPECTIVELY INTERPRET THE LAW TO GET THE SAME RESULT?
OR SHOULD I APPLY THE LAW RIGOROUSLY, AND HOPE TO GET A JUST OUTCOME?
SIGH!
WHAT DO YOU THINK, WOOLF?
ONE BARK FOR NOT GUILTY, TWO FOR GUILTY
WOOF! WOOF!
GUILTY IT IS THEN!

POOR OLD FELLOW, HE'S GETTING OLD AND DEAF THESE DAYS.
ZZZ
HE SLEEPS ALL DAY LONG AND HARDLY WAKES UP EXCEPT FOR HIS DINNER.
ZZZ
HE'S COMPLETELY PAST IT – I DON'T KNOW WHAT'S TO BE DONE WITH HIM.
ZZZ
PROMOTE HIM TO THE HIGH COURT?
POOR CHAP.

IT'S HARD TO TELL WHICH WAY THE JUDGE IS LEANING..
HE'S NOT GIVING MUCH AWAY, IS HE?
HE DIDN'T BAT AN EYELID DURING YOUR CROSS-EXAMINATION.
I WONDER IF HE'S WITH US ON THE LAW?
I WONDER IF HE'S WITH US ON THE FACTS?
I WONDER IF I SHOULD PRUNE THE WISTERIA THIS WEEKEND?

HOW LEGAL REFORM WORKS:
THE SYSTEM IS AWFUL – IT NEEDS CHANGING.
OR AT LEAST... SOME INJUSTICES SHOULD BE REMEDIED.
WE MUST RETAIN THE GOOD ELEMENTS, WHILE REFORMING THE BAD.
BRIEF
WHEN ABLY ADMINISTERED, THE SYSTEM WORKS WELL.
£
ENGLISH JUSTICE IS THE FINEST IN THE WORLD.

I DON'T KNOW WHICH SIDE TO PICK TODAY. WHO SHOULD WIN?
IT'S ALL VERY EVENLY BALANCED. WHAT WOULD YOU DO?
THAT'S OBVIOUS HUMPHREY! YOU SHOULD OBVIOUSLY PICK...
... THE SIDE WITH THE SEXIEST COUNSEL...

M'LUD, THE QUESTION TURNS UPON THE REVERSION OF THE TESTATOR'S ESTATE TO THE EXPECTANT HEIR OF THE ASSIGNEE.
...FURTHER TO THE ORIGINAL DOMICILE OF THE INSURED WHICH WAS SUBJECT TO A LIEN UPON THE ESTATE IN PERSONAM.
...NOTWITHSTANDING THE ABEYANCE OF THE REVISED TRUST.
YOU MIGHT SAY, SIR GEOFFREY, THAT "IN REM POSTERIORE QUAE LEGES SUNT"
HA! HA! HA!
HO! HO! HO!
QUITE A BIT OF FUN WE HAD IN THE CHANCERY DIVISION TODAY.
OH INDEED

YOU HAVE BEEN FOUND GUILTY OF AN ACT OF GROSS PUBLIC INDECENCY.
IN IMPOSING A SENTENCE, I MUST BEAR IN MIND YOUR DISGRACEFUL RECORD OF RE-OFFENDING.
YOU ARE A MENACE TO SOCIETY, AND THE PUBLIC IS ENTITLED TO A REST FROM YOUR ACTIVITIES.
...AND IF YOU EVER DO THAT ON THE CARPET AGAIN, I'LL HAVE YOU COMMITTED.

SOME DAYS I GET SO FED UP WITH BEING A JUDGE.
...SPENDING ALL MY TIME SURROUNDED BY CRIMINALS...
CRIMINAL COURT
EVERY DAY I HAVE TO COME TO WORK AND MEET THE DREGS OF SOCIETY.
...AND THEN I HAVE TO MEET THEIR CLIENTS.

I CAN'T IMAGINE WHY ANYONE WOULD WANT TO BE A HIGH COURT JUDGE NOWADAYS.
TOP QC's REFUSE HIGH COURT
THE PAY IS TERRIBLE, THE PRESS HOUND YOU, AND THE PUBLIC DON'T RESPECT YOU ANY MORE.
YOU EVEN HAVE TO GO ON "POLITICAL CORRECTNESS" TRAINING COURSES! IT'S A THANKLESS TASK.
HMPH!
STILL HAVEN'T BEEN ASKED THEN ?
SIGH!
NO

NEW JUDICIAL ROBES for 2008
① DISTRICT JUDGE
② CROWN COURT JUDGE
③ COURT of APPEAL
④ HOUSE of LORDS.

LOOK, THERE GOES MR JUSTICE HARGREAVES ...JUST SEEING HIM SENDS SHIVERS DOWN MY SPINE!!
HARGREAVES?
THE TERMINATOR? STRIKES FEAR INTO THE HEART OF THE BAR?
THE SAME.
LAST WEEK I SAW HIM TEAR A QC LIMB FROM LIMB!
TERRIFYING MAN.

I PROMISE TO TELL THE TRUTH, THE WHOLE TRUTH, AND NOTHING BUT THE TRUTH.
AS FAR AS I CAN REMEMBER IT
WE PROMISE TO TELL EVASIONS AND HALF-TRUTHS, WITHOUT EVER ACTUALLY TELLING AN UNTRUTH.
I PROMISE TO TRY AND WORK OUT WHICH SIDE IS TELLING THE TRUTH.
I EXERCISE MY RIGHT TO SILENCE AND HOPE NO-ONE FINDS OUT THE REAL TRUTH

I SWEAR TO TELL THE TRUTH, THE WHOLE TRUTH...
... AND NOTHING BUT THE TRUTH.
M'LUD, THE JURY HAVE A QUESTION FOR THE COURT.
WELL... WHAT IS IT?
HOW COME THE LAWYERS NEVER HAVE TO SWEAR TO TELL THE TRUTH?

I SEE THAT THE BAR COUNCIL HAVE CALLED FOR MORE DIVERSITY IN JUDICIAL APPOINTMENTS.
ETHNIC MINORITIES, WOMEN AND PERSONS WITH DISABILITIES ARE ENCOURAGED TO APPLY.
WELL... THAT'S SIR GEOFFREY DONE FOR THEN.
HMM... NOT NECESSARILY.
HAS ANYONE SEEN MY KORAN?

TRUTH in LAW
SIR GEOFFREY, HOW LONG DO YOU INTEND TO BORE ME WITH THIS CASE?
M'LUD, SINCE I AM ON A DAILY RATE... AS LONG AS POSSIBLE.
AND YOU, MR LONG-WIND?
M'LUD, I TOO SEEK THE MAXIMUM PROLIXITY AND DELAY.
I SEE... AND YOUR DEFENCE? THE USUAL NONSENSE?
A WEB OF HALF-TRUTHS AND EVASIONS.
I'LL PUT YOU DOWN FOR A THREE DAY TRIAL... WAKE ME UP AFTER TWO WEEKS WOULD YOU?
...IF WE HAVEN'T TAKEN A MORE LUCRATIVE CASE BY THEN.

I JUST DON'T KNOW HOW TO JUDGE THIS CASE. BOTH SIDES HAVE GOOD ARGUMENTS, AND THE WITNESSES ALL SOUND CONVINCING.
JUDGE'S CHAMBERS
HOW WOULD YOU DECIDE IT?
WELL... LET ME SEE THE WRITTEN SUBMISSIONS.
HMM... YES... JUST AS I THOUGHT.
WHAT?!
A TYPO. I GENERALLY FIND FOR THE PARTY WITH THE FEWEST SPELLING ERRORS

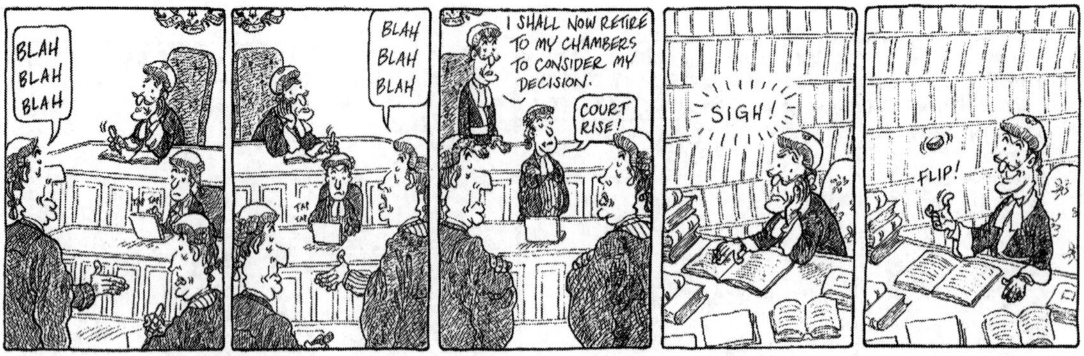
BLAH BLAH BLAH
BLAH BLAH BLAH
I SHALL NOW RETIRE TO MY CHAMBERS TO CONSIDER MY DECISION.
COURT RISE!
SIGH!
FLIP!

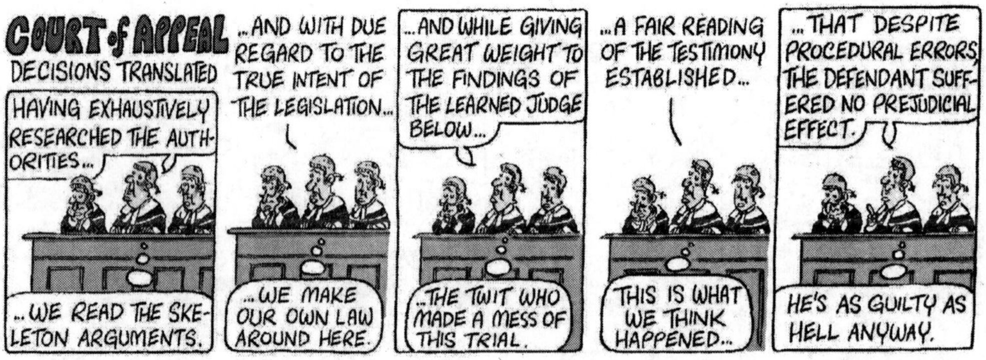
COURT of APPEAL
DECISIONS TRANSLATED
HAVING EXHAUSTIVELY RESEARCHED THE AUTHORITIES...
...WE READ THE SKELETON ARGUMENTS.
...AND WITH DUE REGARD TO THE TRUE INTENT OF THE LEGISLATION...
...WE MAKE OUR OWN LAW AROUND HERE.
...AND WHILE GIVING GREAT WEIGHT TO THE FINDINGS OF THE LEARNED JUDGE BELOW...
...THE TWIT WHO MADE A MESS OF THIS TRIAL.
...A FAIR READING OF THE TESTIMONY ESTABLISHED...
THIS IS WHAT WE THINK HAPPENED...
...THAT DESPITE PROCEDURAL ERRORS, THE DEFENDANT SUFFERED NO PREJUDICIAL EFFECT.
HE'S AS GUILTY AS HELL ANYWAY.

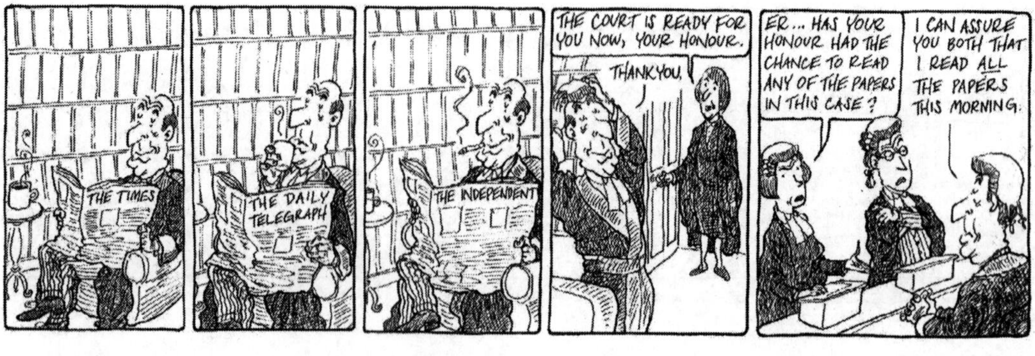
THE TIMES
THE DAILY TELEGRAPH
THE INDEPENDENT
THE COURT IS READY FOR YOU NOW, YOUR HONOUR.
THANK YOU.
ER... HAS YOUR HONOUR HAD THE CHANCE TO READ ANY OF THE PAPERS IN THIS CASE?
I CAN ASSURE YOU BOTH THAT I READ ALL THE PAPERS THIS MORNING.

THIS COURT HAS BEEN CHOSEN TO PILOT THE VERY LATEST IN CASE-MANAGEMENT TECHNOLOGY.
PLIK
IN FRONT OF EACH OF YOU IS A SCREEN, ENABLING YOU TO VIEW TRIAL DOCUMENTS IN REAL TIME, WITHOUT THE NEED FOR COUNTLESS PAPER COPIES.
PLIK PLIK
PLOK
THE WHOLE SYSTEM TOOK SIX MONTHS TO INSTALL AND COST OVER £50,000.
SHAKE
SQUEAK
...AND THIS IS MY FIVE YEAR OLD GRANDSON WHO WILL SHOW US ALL HOW TO TURN IT ON.

CRIME:
the BARRISTER'S PROGRESS
① the STUDENT
I WANT TO BE A CRIMINAL LAWYER SO I CAN DEFEND THE WEAK AGAINST THE STRONG.
LAW
THE JUNIOR BARRISTER
MY CLIENTS AREN'T REALLY GUILTY, THEY'RE JUST UNDER-PRIVILEGED.
THE EMINENT SILK.
WHAT I NEED IS SOME RICHER CRIMINAL CLIENTS.
...WHO CAN AFFORD MY FEES
THE JUDGE
QUITE FRANKLY, THEY'RE OBVIOUSLY ALL GUILTY

I FEAR I MUST RULE AGAINST YOU, MR LONGWIND.
RIDICULOUS. WHAT AN ABSURD DECISION.
I AM PARTLY WITH YOU AND PARTLY AGAINST YOU.
WHAT A MEDIOCRITY
I FIND IN YOUR FAVOUR.
WHAT AN EXCELLENT JUDGE
I PROPOSE WE TAKE A SHORT LUNCHEON ADJOURNMENT-SAY UNTIL MONDAY MORNING.
ONE OF THE FINEST MINDS ON THE BENCH.

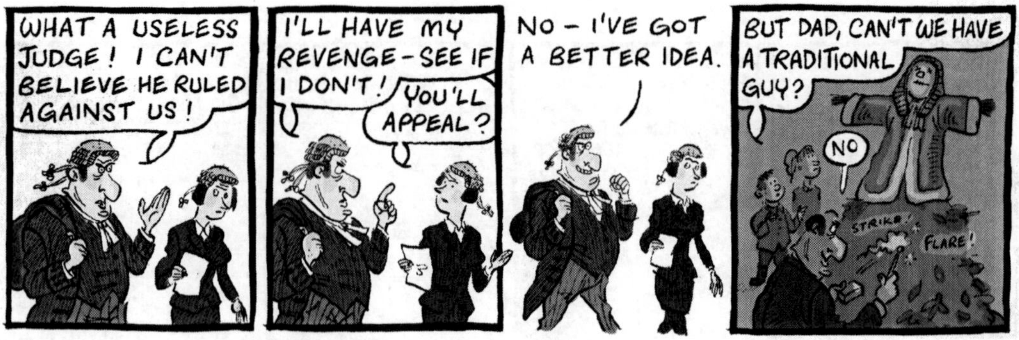
WHAT A USELESS JUDGE! I CAN'T BELIEVE HE RULED AGAINST US!
I'LL HAVE MY REVENGE - SEE IF I DON'T!
YOU'LL APPEAL?
NO - I'VE GOT A BETTER IDEA.
BUT DAD, CAN'T WE HAVE A TRADITIONAL GUY?
NO
STRIKE!
FLARE!

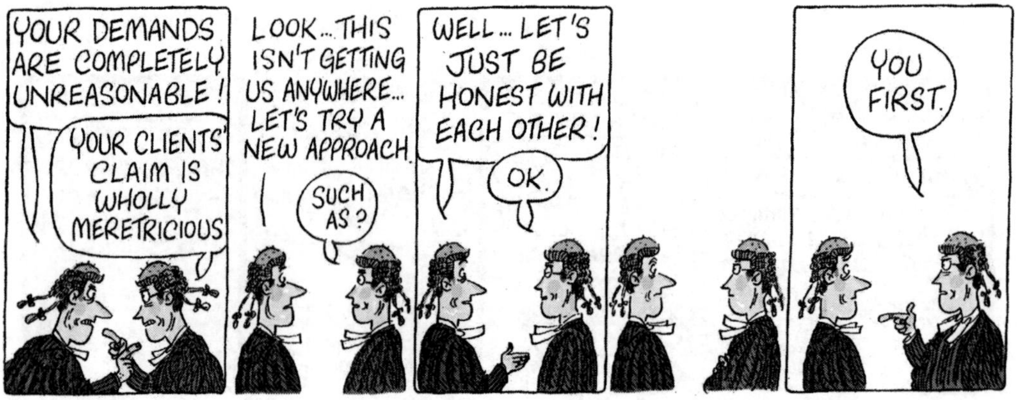
YOUR DEMANDS ARE COMPLETELY UNREASONABLE!
YOUR CLIENTS' CLAIM IS WHOLLY MERETRICIOUS
LOOK... THIS ISN'T GETTING US ANYWHERE... LET'S TRY A NEW APPROACH.
SUCH AS?
WELL... LET'S JUST BE HONEST WITH EACH OTHER!
OK.
YOU FIRST.

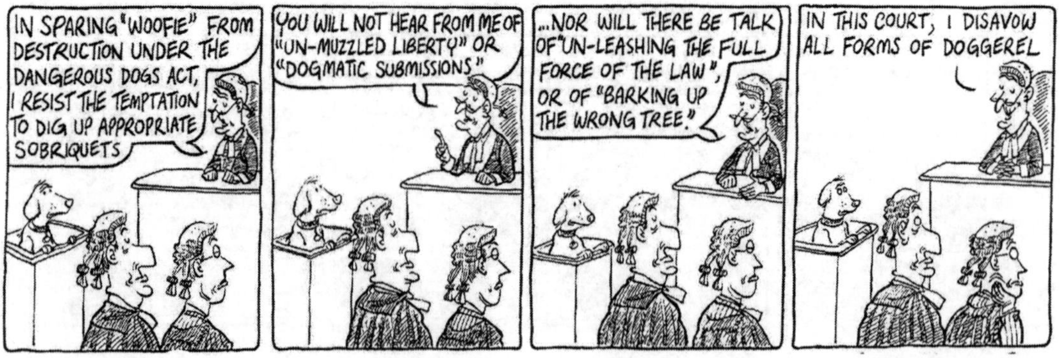
IN SPARING "WOOFIE" FROM DESTRUCTION UNDER THE DANGEROUS DOGS ACT, I RESIST THE TEMPTATION TO DIG UP APPROPRIATE SOBRIQUETS
YOU WILL NOT HEAR FROM ME OF "UN-MUZZLED LIBERTY" OR "DOGMATIC SUBMISSIONS."
...NOR WILL THERE BE TALK OF "UN-LEASHING THE FULL FORCE OF THE LAW", OR OF "BARKING UP THE WRONG TREE."
IN THIS COURT, I DISAVOW ALL FORMS OF DOGGEREL

THESE FRAUD CHARGES ARE SO COMPLEX – IT'S A WONDER ANY JURY CAN UNDERSTAND THEM.

I JUST HOPE THEY CAN GET TO GRIPS WITH ALL THESE PAPERS.

SOME OF THE DOCUMENTS ARE CLEARLY GIVING THEM TROUBLE.

I SWEAR BY ALRIGHTY DOG ...ER...

START AGAIN PLEASE.

SIGH IT'S GOING TO BE A LONG DAY...

AS MEMBERS OF THE NEWLY CONSTITUTED SUPREME COURT, IT'S HIGH TIME WE TOOK A POSITION ON ASSISTED SUICIDE.

ELDERLY PATIENTS WHO NO LONGER WISH TO LIVE MUST BE ENTITLED TO END THEIR OWN LIVES.

IN SOME CASES, DEATH MAY BE PREFERABLE TO LIFE.

...AND IF SIR GEOFFREY DOESN'T END HIS SUB-MISSIONS SOON, I WANT THE RIGHT TO END MINE.

AGREED.

BLAH, BLAH...

BAH! REJECTED AGAIN! SURELY THE LORD CHANCELLOR CAN SEE I WOULD MAKE AN EXCELLENT JUDGE!

WHAT MAKES YOU WANT TO BE ONE SO MUCH, ROLAND?

WHY...TO DISPENSE JUSTICE, OF COURSE.

OH, COME ON.

WELL... TO SERVE QUEEN AND COUNTRY THEN.

MM...HM.

AND THE REAL REASON?

ACCESS TO THE JUDICIAL DINING ROOMS.

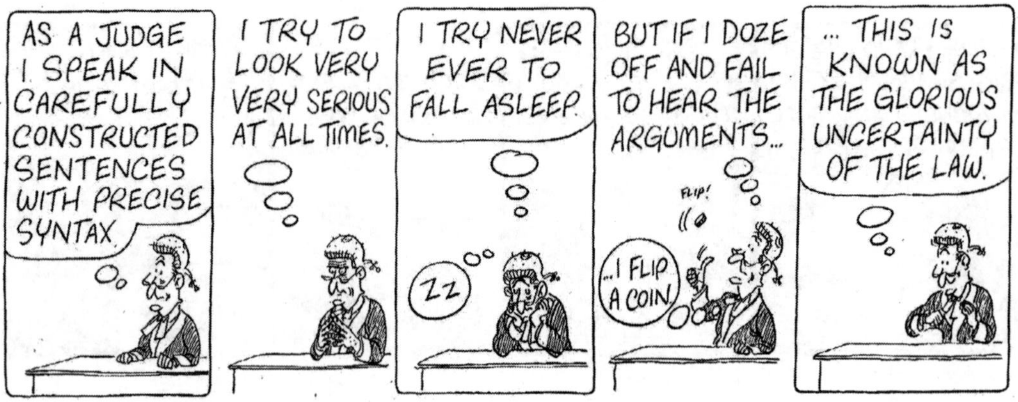
AS A JUDGE I SPEAK IN CAREFULLY CONSTRUCTED SENTENCES WITH PRECISE SYNTAX.
I TRY TO LOOK VERY VERY SERIOUS AT ALL TIMES.
I TRY NEVER EVER TO FALL ASLEEP.
ZZ
BUT IF I DOZE OFF AND FAIL TO HEAR THE ARGUMENTS...
FLIP!
...I FLIP A COIN.
... THIS IS KNOWN AS THE GLORIOUS UNCERTAINTY OF THE LAW.

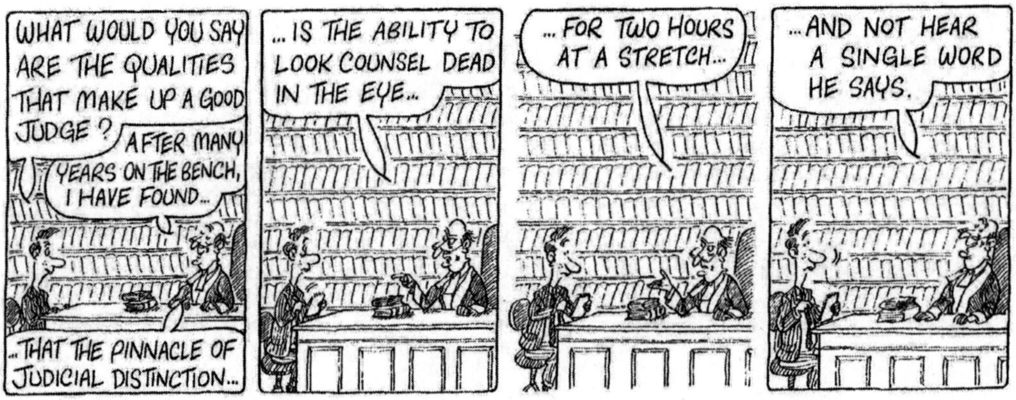
WHAT WOULD YOU SAY ARE THE QUALITIES THAT MAKE UP A GOOD JUDGE?
AFTER MANY YEARS ON THE BENCH, I HAVE FOUND...
...THAT THE PINNACLE OF JUDICIAL DISTINCTION...
... IS THE ABILITY TO LOOK COUNSEL DEAD IN THE EYE...
... FOR TWO HOURS AT A STRETCH...
...AND NOT HEAR A SINGLE WORD HE SAYS.

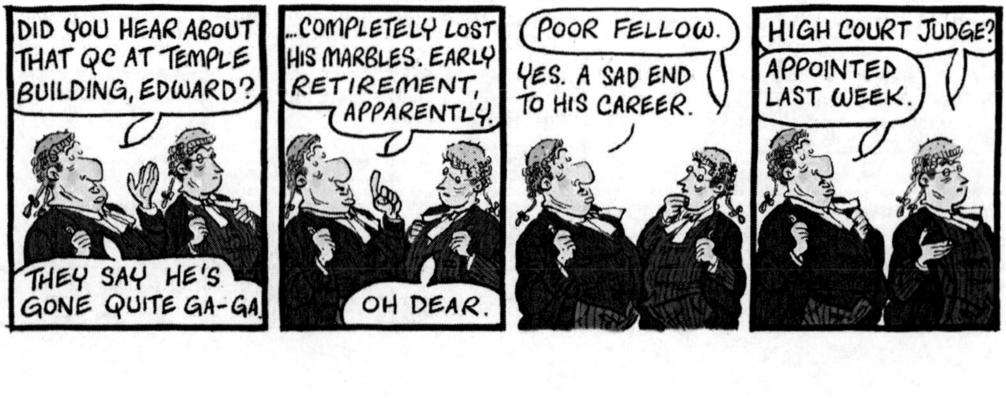
DID YOU HEAR ABOUT THAT QC AT TEMPLE BUILDING, EDWARD?
THEY SAY HE'S GONE QUITE GA-GA
...COMPLETELY LOST HIS MARBLES. EARLY RETIREMENT, APPARENTLY.
OH DEAR.
POOR FELLOW.
YES. A SAD END TO HIS CAREER.
HIGH COURT JUDGE?
APPOINTED LAST WEEK.

ENJOYING YOUR NEW LAPTOP FROM THE LORD CHANCELLORS' DEPARTMENT, HUMPHREY?
THE COMPUTERS ARE FOR JUDICIAL USE ONLY, SIR GEOFFREY.
THEY HELP KEEP US ABREAST OF THE LATEST DEVELOPMENTS.
...LETS US KNOW THE SCORE, SO TO SPEAK.
ANOTHER ENGLAND WICKET FALLS...
BLAH BLAH BLAH
CLONK!

IF THEY'RE GOING TO ABOLISH WIGS FOR CIVIL TRIALS, THEN WHAT ON EARTH ARE WE JUDGES TO WEAR INSTEAD?
HM...
PERHAPS WE SHOULD FOLLOW THE AUSTRALIAN EXAMPLE. THEIR SYSTEM SEEMS TO MAKE SENSIBLE DECISIONS.
WELL... I SUPPOSE IT'S WORTH A TRY...

I'M IN TWO MINDS ABOUT THE WISDOM OF ALLOWING TV CAMERAS INTO OUR COURTS.
OH?
CAMERAS IN COURTS
THE DANGER IS THAT JUSTICE BECOMES SENSATIONALISED!
CAMERAS IN COURT
...BUT THE ADVANTAGE IS THAT WE CAN GET OUR MESSAGE ACROSS TO THE PUBLIC.
QUITE RIGHT
0800 CLAIMS 4 YOU
LAW ADVICE: 1ST HOUR FREE!

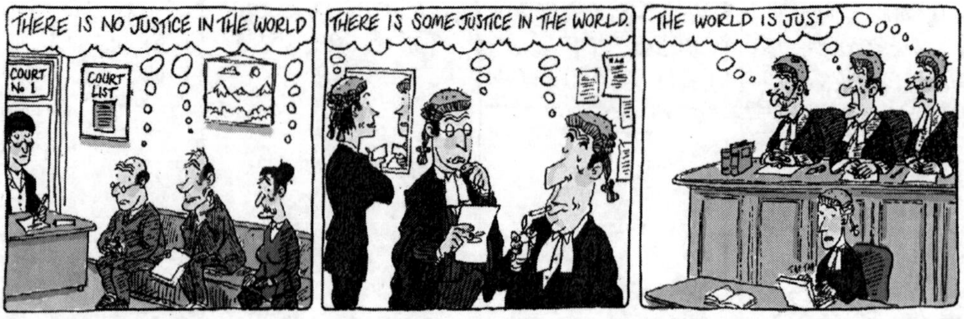
THERE IS NO JUSTICE IN THE WORLD
COURT No 1
COURT LIST
THERE IS SOME JUSTICE IN THE WORLD.
THE WORLD IS JUST

CHAPTER EIGHT
CLIENTS

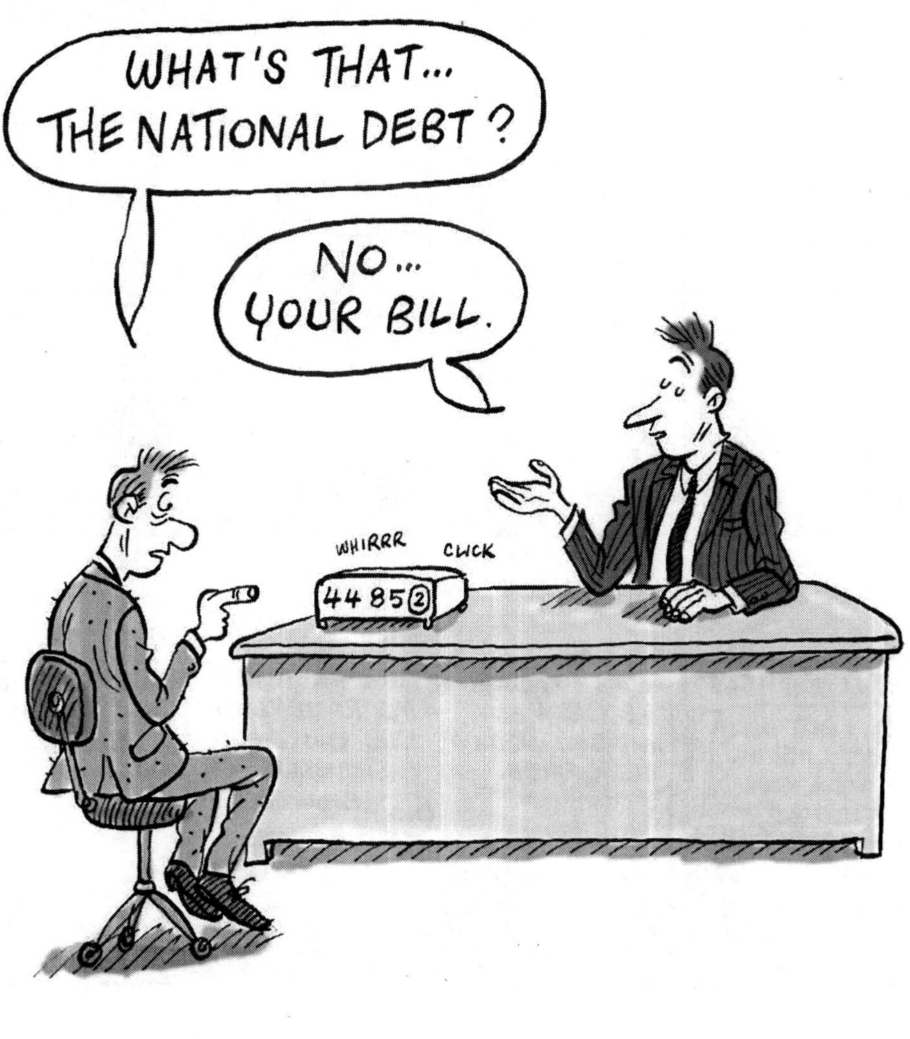
WHAT'S THAT...
THE NATIONAL DEBT?
NO...
YOUR BILL.
WHIRRR
CLICK
44 85②

HELLO MR SPROCKETT, I'M YOUR SOLICITOR, RICHARD LOOPHOLE... DO SIT DOWN AND TELL ME ABOUT YOUR CASE
RING! RING!
EXCUSE ME A MOMENT...
AH YES... TELL THE COURT WE'LL FILE TOMORROW...
...SO HOW CAN I HELP YOU, MR SPROCKETT?
WELL, I...
KNOCK! KNOCK!
HELLO RICHARD...
OH... PARDON ME...
UM...
...LEAVE THOSE RIGHT THERE
CLIENT SATISFACTION IS OUR NUMBER ONE...
RING! RING!
ER...
ONE MOMENT...
TELL COUNSEL I'LL BE RIGHT WITH HIM.
THANKS FOR COMING IN MR SPROCKETT. IF THERE'S ANYTHING ELSE...
I...
RING! RING!

WELL MR SPROCKET, YOU'VE WON YOUR CASE, BUT I'M AFRAID IT'S SOMETHING OF A PYRRHIC VICTORY.
AFTER DISBURSEMENTS, RETAINERS, COSTS, FEES, AND COURT EXPENSES, YOU WILL RECEIVE NOTHING.
NOTHING AT ALL?!?
BUT THEN... WHAT GOOD HAS ALL OF THIS DONE ME?
YOU HAVE BEEN A GOOD CLIENT TO ME MR SPROCKET.
...BUT I MUST SAY YOU SHOW A SURPRISING IGNORANCE OF THE PURPOSES OF LITIGATION

SO HOW CAN I HELP?
WELL, I GOT INTO A FIGHT WITH MY BOSS, AND KNOCKED HIM OUT COLD.
THEN I NICKED THE CASH BOX AND SMASHED UP THE OFFICE.
SO... YOU WANT ME TO DEFEND YOU ON THE CRIMINAL CHARGES?
NO
I WANT YOU TO SUE THEM FOR UNFAIR DISMISSAL.

JOINT CUSTODY IS TOTALLY UNACCEPTABLE.
YOUR CLIENT'S DEMANDS ARE RIDICULOUS
YOUR CLIENT IS HIDING ASSETS
THERE IS NO ROOM FOR COMPROMISE HERE
GRRR!! !!!
MAYBE WE SHOULD GET BACK TOGETHER...

the CLiENT CONFERENCE translated
MR SPROCKET, YOURS IS A MOST INTERESTING* CASE.
*LUCRATIVE.
...WHICH COULD GO ONE OF TWO WAYS...
*I HAVEN'T THE SLIGHTEST IDEA WHICH.
BUT MOST OF ALL I'D LIKE TO REASSURE YOU...*
*HAVE YOU NOTICED I'M BUSKING?
...THAT I HAVEN'T LOST A CASE IN TEN YEARS.
*I SETTLE ALL MY CASES LONG BEFORE THEY GET TO COURT.

HOW MUCH WILL IT COST TO FIGHT MY CASE, MR LOOPHOLE?
WELL, MY RATE IS THREE HUNDRED POUNDS AN HOUR
I... I SEE...
...PLUS VAT AT SEVENTEEN AND A HALF PERCENT.
WELL, THAT SHOULD BE FINE, THEN.
...I SUPPOSE.
...AS LONG AS YOU CAN DO THE ENTIRE JOB IN UNDER TWENTY MINUTES.

LITIGATION: a GUIDE
① HOW THE CASE WAS EXPLAINED TO THE CLIENT.
YOU HAVE A VERY STRONG CASE, MR SPROCKET.
② HOW IT PROGRESSED.
I RATE OUR CHANCES AROUND 50 : 50.
③ HOW IT TURNED OUT.
I REJECT THIS CLAIM AND AWARD INDEMNITY COSTS AGAINST THE CLAIMANT.
④ HOW THE CLIENT WAS BILLED.

BUT SHOULD I ACCEPT THEIR OFFER, SIR GEOFFREY?
I'M AFRAID THAT'S A DECISION FOR YOU, MR SPROCKETT
LITIGATION IS A RISKY BUSINESS
INDEED
YOU CAN NEVER TELL WHAT A JUDGE WILL DO WITH A CASE LIKE THIS.
SOMETIMES YOU WIN, SOMETIMES YOU LOSE
WHAT DID THE LAWYERS ADVISE, DEAR?
ER... I'M NOT SURE
SCRATCH

IF I STEAL £50, AND GET CAUGHT, I CAN'T AFFORD A LAWYER AND I GO TO PRISON FOR THREE MONTHS.
BUT IF I STEAL £500, I CAN AFFORD A BRIEF, AND MAYBE HE'LL GET ME A LIGHTER SENTENCE.
NOW IF I STEAL £50,000, I CAN BUY A TOP DRAWER BARRISTER LIKE YOURSELF, AND HE'LL GET ME OFF.
BUT IF I STEAL £5,000,000, IT'S NOT EVEN CALLED STEALING! IT'S "EMBEZZLEMENT."

WHICH LAWYER IS RIGHT FOR YOU?
I'M SORRY MR SPROCKET, BUT YOUR CLAIM IS VERY UNLIKELY TO SUCCEED.
I WANT A SECOND OPINION.
I'M AFRAID I MUST ADVISE THAT YOUR CASE IS RATHER WEAK.
I WANT A THIRD OPINION...
... REGRETTABLY, THE CHANCES OF SUCCESS ARE SMALL ...
I WANT A FOURTH OPINION.
'COURSE, I'M NOT AN EXPERT IN THIS AREA OF LAW, BUT I EXPECT YOU'VE GOT A DECENT CHANCE.
GREAT! I'D LIKE TO GET STARTED RIGHT AWAY!

I'M VERY SORRY, MR SPROCKET, BUT YOUR CASE HAS TAKEN A DISASTROUS TURN FOR THE WORSE.
IF YOU LOSE, YOU FACE A MASSIVE PRISON SENTENCE AND A HUGE FINE.
EVEN IF YOU WIN, THE LEGAL COSTS ALONE WILL PROBABLY BANKRUPT YOU.
APRIL FOOL!
JUST KIDDING!

I'M AFRAID GLYNDBOURNE IS NOT WHAT IT WAS, EDWARD. LOOK AT ALL THESE SPIVS AND SHADY DEALERS.
TOO MANY "BELOW STAIRS" TYPES IF YOU ASK ME. WHO DO THESE PEOPLE THINK THEY ARE ANYWAY?
HALLO SIR GEOFFREY! FANCY MEETIN' YOU HERE!
—YOUR CLIENTS, PERHAPS?
NICE WORK GETTING ME OFF ON THEM MONEYLAUNDERING CHARGES, GEOFF!
CRINGE

BUT WILL WE WIN, SIR GEOFFREY?
I'M AFRAID THAT THERE ARE MANY VARIABLES, MR SPROCKET.
THE PERFORMANCE OF THE WITNESSES, THE MOOD OF THE JUDGE, THE LUCK OF THE DICE...
...OR... AS WE SAY AT THE BAR...
NIHIL CERTUM NISI OMNIA INCERTA.
ER... WHAT DOES THAT MEAN, EXACTLY?
IF WE LOSE, IT'S BECAUSE YOUR CASE WAS ROTTEN FROM THE START. IF WE WIN, IT'S BECAUSE I'M A SUPERB ADVOCATE.

I'M AFRAID THAT THIS IS LIKELY TO BE AN EXPENSIVE DIVORCE FOR YOU, MR SPROCKET.
YOU MEAN... MY WIFE WILL GET HALF OF MY FORTUNE?
OH NO... NOT THAT MUCH.
PHEW... THAT'S A RELIEF.
NO, WE GET HALF. YOU AND YOUR WIFE SPLIT THE REST.

ALL THE LARGE CITY LAW FIRMS ARE WRITING TO THEIR CLIENTS, SEEKING TO EXCLUDE LIABILITY FOR ALL WORK DONE BETWEEN MIDNIGHT AND 6AM.
...AND I THINK IT'S HIGH TIME THAT OUR FIRM DID THE SAME.
BUT RICHARD, WE ALMOST NEVER WORK THAT LATE.
HM... I SUPPOSE YOU'RE RIGHT. WELL... IN THAT CASE...
...LET'S EXCLUDE LIABILITY FOR ALL WORK DONE AFTER LUNCHTIME.
EXCELLENT PLAN.

I'M AFRAID YOUR CASE IS VERY WEAK MR SPROCKET, UTTERLY WITHOUT MERIT.
YOU HAVE NO WITNESSES TO CONFIRM YOUR STORY, AND THE AUTHORITIES ARE AGAINST YOU.
BUT I AM GLAD TO SAY THERE IS ONE SAVING GRACE,
WHICH REDEEMS YOUR OTHER-WISE HOPELESS POSITION.
... THE EXCELLENT QUALITY OF YOUR LEGAL ADVICE.

YOU HAVE REACHED THE LAW OFFICES OF PAYE, CASH & PRAYE. PRESS "1" FOR DIVORCE, "2" FOR PERSONAL INJURY, "3" FOR CRIME...
IF YOU ARE A VEXATIOUS LITIGANT, PRESS "4" FURIOUSLY AND REPEATEDLY...
CONTINGENCY FEE CLIENTS PLEASE HOLD INDEFINITELY. YOU HAVE NOT BEEN CHARGED FOR THIS CALL...
IF YOU HAVE A COMPLAINT ABOUT OUR BILL, PLEASE LEAVE YOUR NAME AND NUMBER AND NO-ONE WILL GET BACK TO YOU.

WHAT IS YOUR LEAST EXPENSIVE FEE, MR LOOPHOLE ?
£100 – TO ANSWER 3 QUESTIONS.
£100? ISN'T THAT A LOT OF MONEY FOR JUST 3 QUESTIONS?
ARGUABLY
WHAT'S YOUR FINAL QUESTION?
FEE NOTE
£100

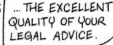

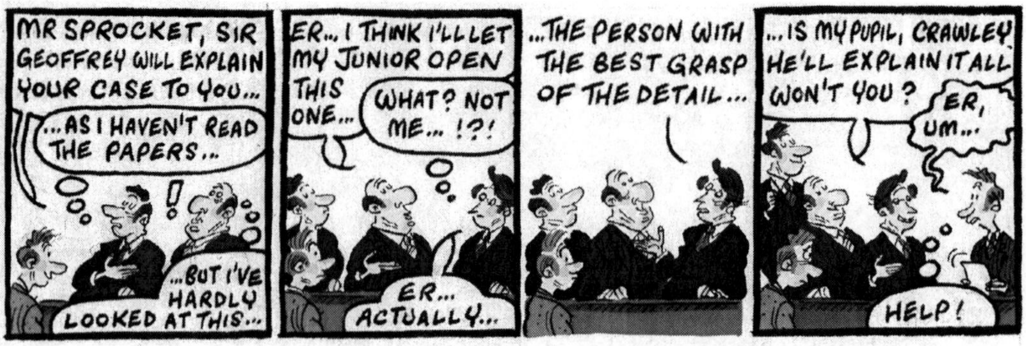
MR SPROCKET, SIR GEOFFREY WILL EXPLAIN YOUR CASE TO YOU...
...AS I HAVEN'T READ THE PAPERS...
!
...BUT I'VE HARDLY LOOKED AT THIS...
ER... I THINK I'LL LET MY JUNIOR OPEN THIS ONE...
WHAT? NOT ME... !?!
ER... ACTUALLY...
...THE PERSON WITH THE BEST GRASP OF THE DETAIL...
...IS MY PUPIL, CRAWLEY HE'LL EXPLAIN IT ALL WON'T YOU ?
ER, UM...
HELP!

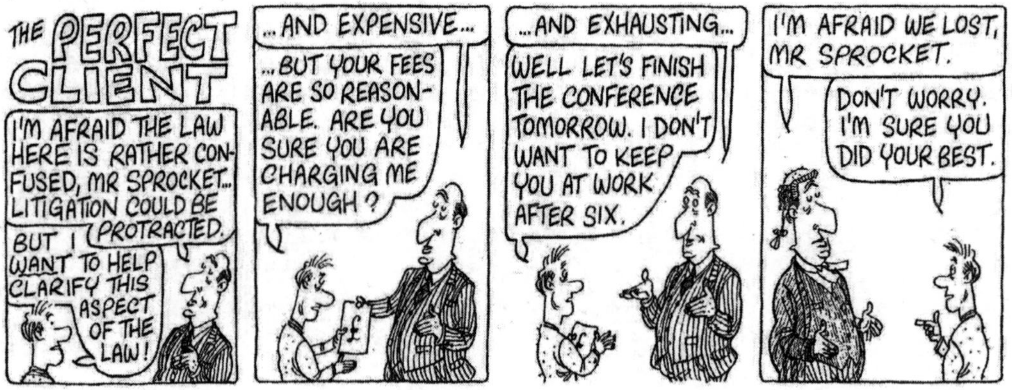
THE PERFECT CLIENT
I'M AFRAID THE LAW HERE IS RATHER CONFUSED, MR SPROCKET... LITIGATION COULD BE PROTRACTED.
BUT I WANT TO HELP CLARIFY THIS ASPECT OF THE LAW!
...AND EXPENSIVE...
...BUT YOUR FEES ARE SO REASONABLE. ARE YOU SURE YOU ARE CHARGING ME ENOUGH ?
...AND EXHAUSTING...
WELL LET'S FINISH THE CONFERENCE TOMORROW. I DON'T WANT TO KEEP YOU AT WORK AFTER SIX.
I'M AFRAID WE LOST, MR SPROCKET.
DON'T WORRY. I'M SURE YOU DID YOUR BEST.

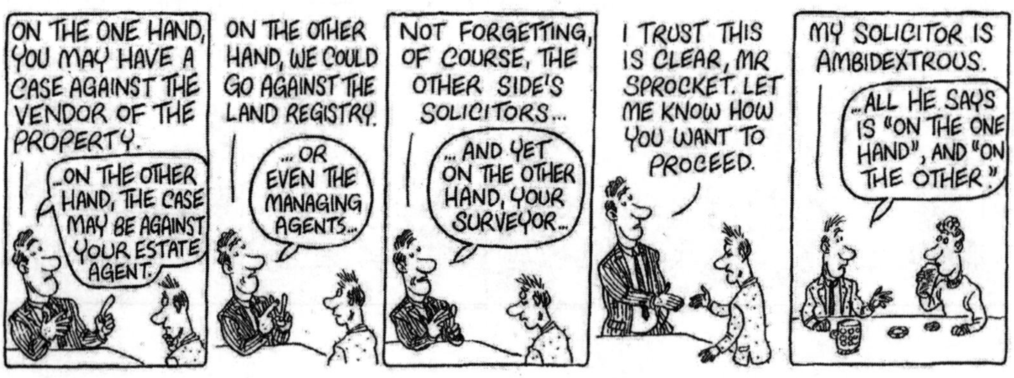
ON THE ONE HAND, YOU MAY HAVE A CASE AGAINST THE VENDOR OF THE PROPERTY.
...ON THE OTHER HAND, THE CASE MAY BE AGAINST YOUR ESTATE AGENT.
ON THE OTHER HAND, WE COULD GO AGAINST THE LAND REGISTRY.
...OR EVEN THE MANAGING AGENTS...
NOT FORGETTING, OF COURSE, THE OTHER SIDE'S SOLICITORS...
...AND YET ON THE OTHER HAND, YOUR SURVEYOR...
I TRUST THIS IS CLEAR, MR SPROCKET. LET ME KNOW HOW YOU WANT TO PROCEED.
MY SOLICITOR IS AMBIDEXTROUS.
...ALL HE SAYS IS "ON THE ONE HAND", AND "ON THE OTHER."

DON'T WORRY, MR SPROCKET, WE'LL TEAR THE OTHER SIDE LIMB FROM LIMB.
WE'LL RIP THEM TO PIECES... WE'LL FLAY THEM ALIVE!
WE'LL DESTROY THEM AND GRIND THEM INTO THE DUST!
AH, GERALD, LOVELY TO SEE YOU OLD CHAP. I'M SURE WE CAN SETTLE THIS ONE IN A GENTLEMANLY FASHION.
AS ALWAYS.

CLIENT ON LINE ONE, RACHEL!
I'VE GOT ANOTHER ONE ON LINE TWO!
RING!
YES... WE'RE WORKING ON YOUR CASE NOW
TOMORROW, I PROMISE, YES!
YES, BY MONDAY, DEFINITELY!
THE TROUBLE WITH KEEPING CLIENTS HAPPY...
...IS THAT I NEVER GET A CHANCE TO GET ANY ACTUAL WORK DONE.
RING! RING!
RING! RING!
WHERE IS THAT CLIENT REPORT?

I'M SORRY, BUT THAT'S NOT AN ACCEPTABLE SETTLEMENT OFFER.
£100,000 IS JUST NOT ENOUGH.
AFTER ALL...
MY CLIENT NEEDS SOMETHING TOO.

NO TIME TO READ THE CORRESPONDENCE FILE...
...NEVER DONE THIS AREA OF LAW BEFORE...
NO BACK-UP FROM THE PARTNER IN CHARGE, AND A CLIENT CONF-ERENCE IN TEN MINUTES
MR SPROCKET, RACHEL HERE WILL EXPLAIN EVERY-THING TO YOU...

I'M SORRY MR SPROCKET, WE DID OUR BEST FOR YOU
BUT WHAT AM I TO DO? I'LL BE RUINED!
YOU HAVE MY SYMPATHY. IF THERE IS ANYTHING WE CAN DO TO HELP, DO LET US KNOW
WELL, YOU COULD REDUCE YOUR FEE!
THAT WOULD HELP!
!
AH... HA! HA!
VERY GOOD MR SPROCKET
I... I'M SORRY... I DON'T KNOW WHAT CAME OVER ME!
AT LEAST YOU'VE NOT LOST YOUR SENSE OF HUMOUR

HOW TO EXPLAIN TO YOUR CLIENT THAT YOU LOST HIS CASE:
I'M AFRAID, MR SPROCKET, THAT WE SIMPLY GOT THE WRONG JUDGE.
WELL, OF THE TEN ISSUES TO BE TRIED, WE WON NINE OF THEM.
CONGRATULATIONS.
THIS IS JUST THE FIRST SKIRMISH. THE CASE NOW GOES TO THE COURT OF APPEAL.
THE BARRISTER ON THE OTHER SIDE WAS AT SCHOOL WITH THE JUDGE, AND WHAT CAN YOU DO ABOUT THAT?

WHAT WOULD YOU CHARGE TO REPRESENT ME FOR ARMED ROBBERY?
WELL, LET'S SEE... I'D NEED A £5,000 RETAINER...
...AND AT £200 PER HOUR, A TRIAL MIGHT COME TO ABOUT... SAY... £10,000.
DO YOU TAKE CASH?
ER, YES...
CAN YOU HANG ON A COUPLE OF HOURS?
...OK...
...BUT WHERE ARE YOU GOING?
...TO DO THE ROBBERY.
I'LL BE BACK LATER.

HOW IS YOUR LAWYER WORKING OUT?
HORRIBLE! I HATE HIM!
ONE OF THE HARDEST, MOST MEAN-SPIRITED PEOPLE I'VE EVER MET!
SO ARE YOU GOING TO GET RID OF HIM?
NO WAY!
HE TERRIFIES THE OTHER SIDE EVEN MORE THAN HE DOES ME!

A CONTINGENCY FEE IS VERY SIMPLE, MR SPROCKETT. YOU DON'T HAVE TO PAY ME A PENNY UP FRONT.
IF YOU LOSE, I GET NOTHING.
AND IF I WIN?
YOU GET NOTHING.
SCRATCH

I'M AFRAID THAT THE EVIDENCE AGAINST YOU IS QUITE OVER-WHELMING.
THE CROWN HAVE PERSUASIVE WITNESSES AND YOU HAVE NO ALIBI.
IS THERE ANY POSSIBLE DEFENCE WE CAN MAKE TO THESE CHARGES?
ER... I'M VERY FAMOUS AND I PLAY FOR ENGLAND?
THAT SHOULD DO NICELY.
THOUGHT SO.

FOUR (TRUE) THINGS YOU WON'T HEAR FROM YOUR LAWYER
ACTUALLY, MR SPROCKET, WE LOST YOUR CASE DUE TO MY SHODDY WORK.
I DECIDED TO INCREASE YOUR BILL BECAUSE (a) YOU CAN AFFORD IT, and (b) I DON'T LIKE YOU.
YOU KNOW... DIXON & Co DOWN THE ROAD ARE MUCH BETTER AT THIS TYPE OF CASE.
DON'T WORRY, I'VE GOT PLENTY OF CASH ON ME AND I ABSOLUTELY INSIST ON PAYING FOR LUNCH.

BAD DAY, RICHARD?
SOME CLIENTS ARE JUST IMPOSSIBLE. THIS ONE WON'T PAY HIS BILL.
WE SAVED HIM MILLIONS OF POUNDS IN BACK TAXES, PENALTIES, AND FEES HE OWED TO THE REVENUE.
IN THE END, HE GOT OFF WITHOUT PAYING A PENNY.
AND NOW, BELIEVE IT OR NOT, HE WON'T PAY THE MONEY HE OWES US!
THE INGRATE!

...BUT SHOULD I ACCEPT THE OTHER SIDE'S OFFER, SIR GEOFFREY?
THAT DEPENDS
YOU SHOULD ACCEPT THEIR OFFER ONLY IF YOU FEEL SATISFIED THAT THE CHANCES OF SUING AND NOT LOSING ARE NO GREATER THAN THE POSSIBILITY OF NOT SUING AND ACCEPTING AN OFFER WHICH IS NOT HIGH ENOUGH.
IT REALLY IS AS SIMPLE AS THAT, MR SPROCKET

MR SPROCKET, WE'VE SUCCESSFULLY CHALLENGED THE INLAND REVENUE'S CLAIM FOR UNPAID TAX
THEY HAVE AGREED TO WAIVE THE EXTRA £2,000 THEY WERE CLAIMING.
WE'RE VERY PLEASED WITH THIS EXCELLENT OUTCOME.
...SO HERE'S OUR BILL FOR £5,000.

CHAPTER NINE
LAWYERS AT HOME

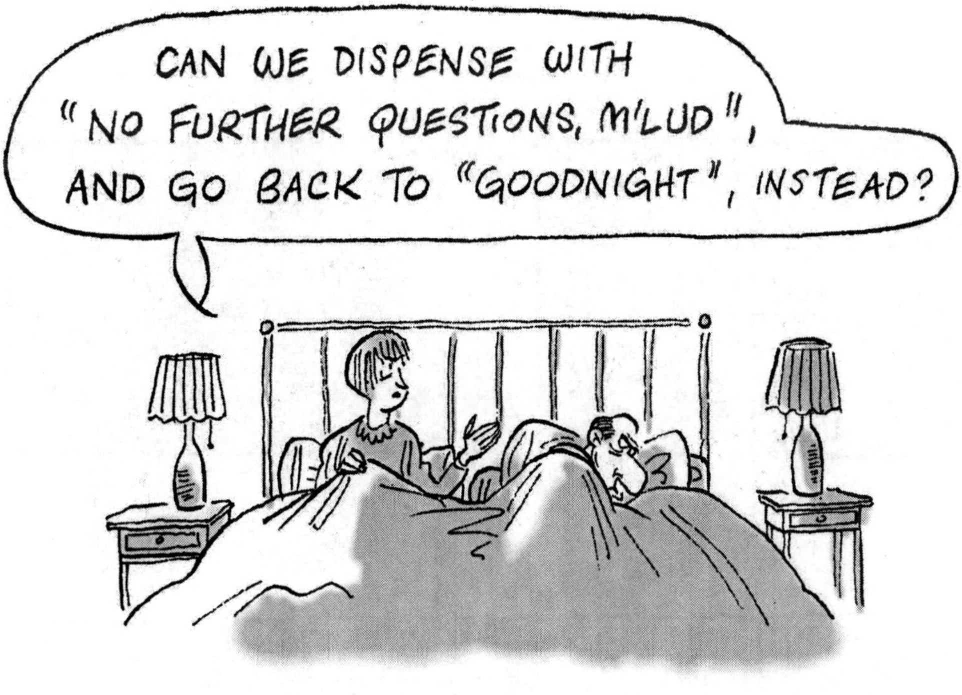
CAN WE DISPENSE WITH "NO FURTHER QUESTIONS, M'LUD", AND GO BACK TO "GOODNIGHT", INSTEAD?

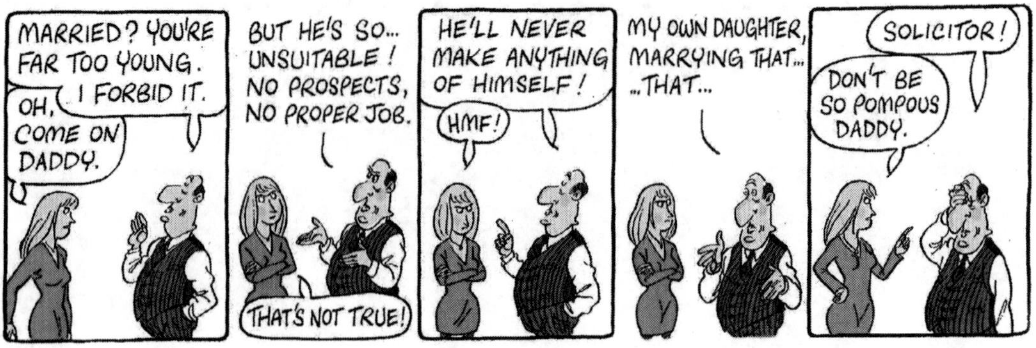
MARRIED? YOU'RE FAR TOO YOUNG. I FORBID IT.
OH, COME ON DADDY.
BUT HE'S SO... UNSUITABLE! NO PROSPECTS, NO PROPER JOB.
THAT'S NOT TRUE!
HE'LL NEVER MAKE ANYTHING OF HIMSELF!
HMF!
MY OWN DAUGHTER, MARRYING THAT... ...THAT...
SOLICITOR!
DON'T BE SO POMPOUS DADDY.

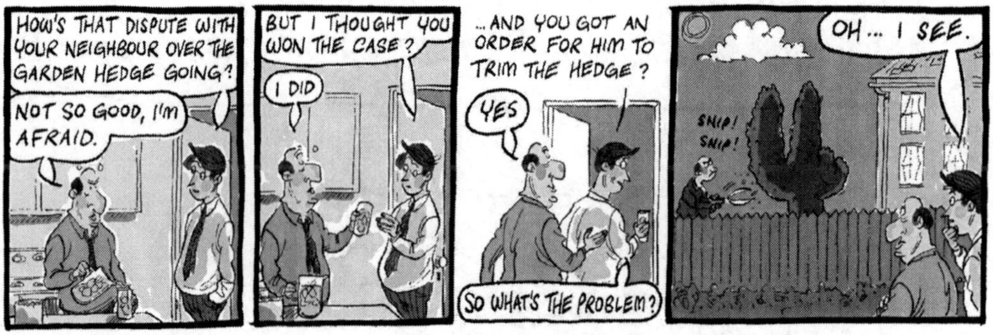
HOW'S THAT DISPUTE WITH YOUR NEIGHBOUR OVER THE GARDEN HEDGE GOING?
NOT SO GOOD, I'M AFRAID.
BUT I THOUGHT YOU WON THE CASE?
I DID
...AND YOU GOT AN ORDER FOR HIM TO TRIM THE HEDGE?
YES
SO WHAT'S THE PROBLEM?
SNIP! SNIP!
OH... I SEE.

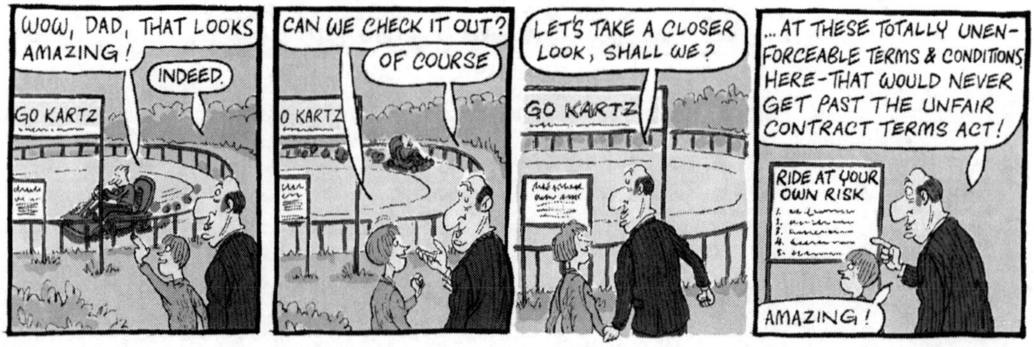
WOW, DAD, THAT LOOKS AMAZING!
INDEED.
GO KARTZ
CAN WE CHECK IT OUT?
OF COURSE
LET'S TAKE A CLOSER LOOK, SHALL WE?
GO KARTZ
...AT THESE TOTALLY UNENFORCEABLE TERMS & CONDITIONS HERE - THAT WOULD NEVER GET PAST THE UNFAIR CONTRACT TERMS ACT!
RIDE AT YOUR OWN RISK
AMAZING!

VALENTINE GIFTS FOR LAWYERS
HMV AND JESSOPS GIFT CARD*
HMV £100
JESSOPS £200
*INSOLVENCY SPECIALISTS ONLY.
ROMANTIC DINNER FOR ONE, "AL DESKO"
SIGH
SINGLE MILK CHOCOLATE TRUFFLE*
*DEEMED TO BE A PERMISSIBLE GIFT UNDER SECTIONS 1-5 OF THE BRIBERY ACT, 2010
"BROKEN HEART" BOX OF CHOCS*
* FOR DIVORCE LAWYERS ONLY.

TO MY VALENTINE, THE MOST BEAUTIFUL WOMAN IN THE WORLD
I WILL LOVE YOU FOREVER
from ?
XXX
OOO
P.S
WITHOUT PREJUDICE TO THE FOREGOING, THIS RELEASE CONTAINS FORWARD-LOOKING STATEMENTS, WHICH ARE BASED UPON A NUMBER OF ASSUMPTIONS. ACTUAL RESULTS MAY BE MATERIALLY DIFFERENT FROM THOSE EXPRESSED OR IMPLIED HEREIN.

I'M AFRAID, YOUNG MAN, THAT YOUR WORK HAS BEEN SOMETHING OF A DISAPPOINTMENT LATELY.
YOU MUST TRY HARDER IF YOU WANT A SUCCESSFUL CAREER AT THE BAR.
DO I MAKE MYSELF CLEAR?
YES, DADDY.

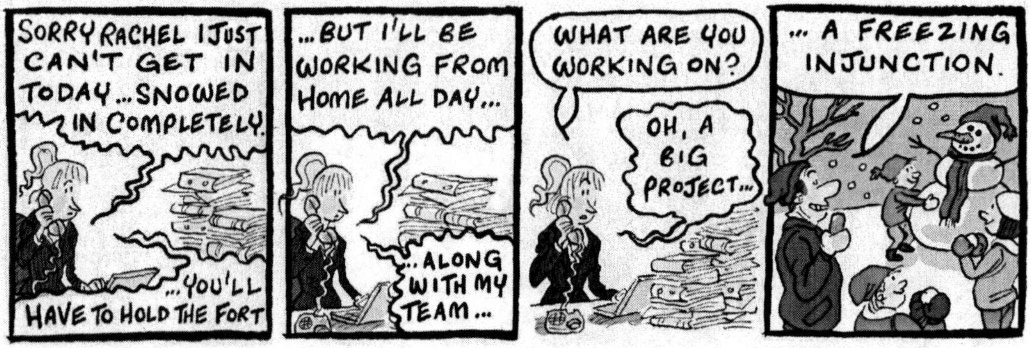
SORRY RACHEL I JUST CAN'T GET IN TODAY ... SNOWED IN COMPLETELY.
... YOU'LL HAVE TO HOLD THE FORT
... BUT I'LL BE WORKING FROM HOME ALL DAY ...
... ALONG WITH MY TEAM ...
WHAT ARE YOU WORKING ON?
OH, A BIG PROJECT ...
... A FREEZING INJUNCTION.

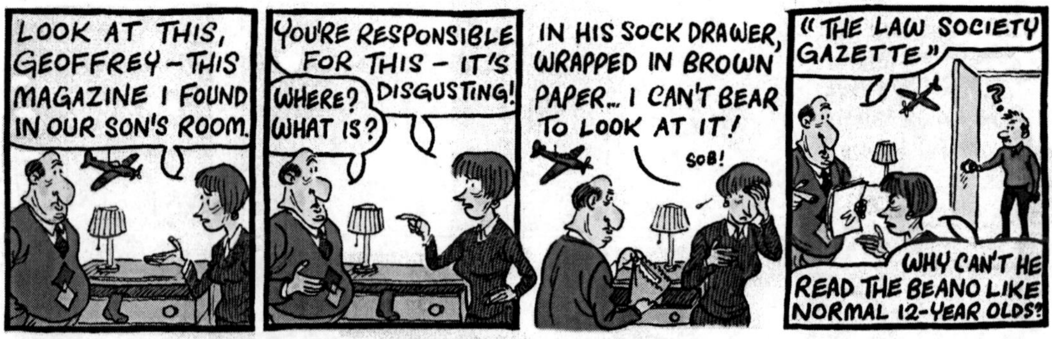
LOOK AT THIS, GEOFFREY - THIS MAGAZINE I FOUND IN OUR SON'S ROOM.
YOU'RE RESPONSIBLE FOR THIS - IT'S DISGUSTING!
WHERE? WHAT IS?
IN HIS SOCK DRAWER, WRAPPED IN BROWN PAPER ... I CAN'T BEAR TO LOOK AT IT!
SOB!
"THE LAW SOCIETY GAZETTE"
?
WHY CAN'T HE READ THE BEANO LIKE NORMAL 12-YEAR OLDS?

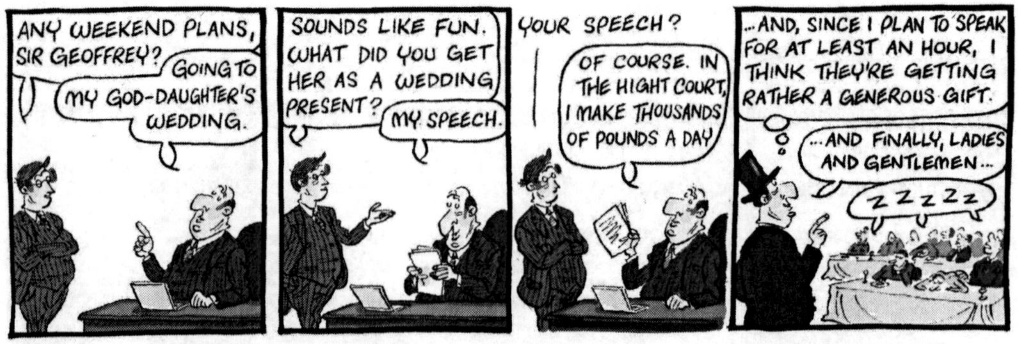
ANY WEEKEND PLANS, SIR GEOFFREY?
GOING TO MY GOD-DAUGHTER'S WEDDING.
SOUNDS LIKE FUN. WHAT DID YOU GET HER AS A WEDDING PRESENT?
MY SPEECH.
YOUR SPEECH?
OF COURSE. IN THE HIGHT COURT, I MAKE THOUSANDS OF POUNDS A DAY
... AND, SINCE I PLAN TO SPEAK FOR AT LEAST AN HOUR, I THINK THEY'RE GETTING RATHER A GENEROUS GIFT.
... AND FINALLY, LADIES AND GENTLEMEN ...
Z Z z Z z

ENGAGED TO BE MARRIED? DARLING THAT'S WONDERFUL!
THANKS DADDY.
...THOUGH YOU MUST ASK THE RIGHT QUESTIONS OF YOUR INTENDED.
SUCH AS?
SUCH AS... "IS THIS THE MAN..."
... I INTEND TO SUE FOR ALIMONY IN TEN YEARS' TIME?

LAWYERS' CHAT-UP LINES
① THE ACTUARY
YOU KNOW, I CAN CALCULATE YOUR EXACT LIFE EXPECTANCY WITHIN 14 MONTHS.
THE PERSONAL INJURY LAWYER.
DID YOU EVER WONDER WHAT YOU MIGHT GET IF YOU WERE RENDERED QUADRAPALEGIC?
PROPERTY LAWYER.
WOULD YOU LIKE TO COME BACK TO MY ASSURED SHORT-HOLD PREMISES?
LITIGATION LAWYER
ER...BEFORE I BUY YOU A DRINK, WOULD YOU MIND SIGNING THIS DISCLAIMER?

TO PRISONER NUMBER 172459X BRIXTON PRISON, LONDON.
DEAR SIR, I REGRET THAT THE COURT OF APPEAL HAVE AGAIN DENIED YOUR APPLICATION FOR A RE-TRIAL ON CHARGES OF ARSON AND ROBBERY.
PS. HAPPY FATHER'S DAY, FROM YOUR LOVING SON. XXX

I'M SORRY BUT I MUST ADVISE YOU OF THE WEAKNESS OF YOUR CASE AGAINST YOUR LANDLORD.

THE PENALTY FOR NON-PAYMENT OF RENT COULD BE EVICTION UNDER THE LANDLORD AND TENANT ACT.

YOUR ONLY CHOICE IS TO PAY THE RENT ARREARS IMMEDIATELY.

... JUST BECAUSE YOU'RE LOSING, GEOFFREY.

IT'S ONLY A GAME, DADDY.

HMF!

MONOPOLY

DEAR VALUED CLIENT, OUR RECORDS SHOW THAT THREE YEARS HAVE PASSED SINCE YOUR LAST WILL OR CODICIL.

TAP TAP TAP

WE RECOMMEND FREQUENT REVISIONS IN ORDER TO MINIMISE ESTATE TAXES.

TAP TAP

PLEASE CALL MY SECRETARY AT YOUR CONVENIENCE TO SET UP AN APPOINTMENT.

TAP TAP TAP

P.S.

TAP

HAPPY MOTHER'S DAY! LOVE, YOUR SON, RICHARD. XXX OOO

TAP TAP TAP

BEDTIME STORIES *for Lawyers*

I CAN'T SLEEP

IT'S 3 am... TRY COUNTING SHEEP.

IT DOESN'T WORK

TAKE A PILL

I DON'T LIKE PILLS... WHY DON'T YOU TELL ME ABOUT YOUR LATEST CASE?

MY CASE?

ER... WELL... IT ALL TURNS ON SECTION 13(a) OF THE APPENDIX TO THE UPDATE TO THE STATUTORY REGULATIONS...

OF COURSE, IT HAS TO BE SEEN IN THE CONTEXT OF JUDICIAL OBITER DICTA...

ZZZ

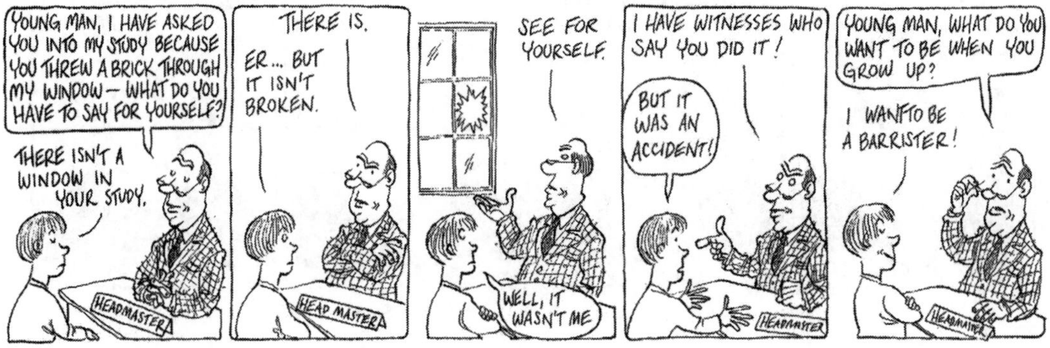

YOUNG MAN, I HAVE ASKED YOU INTO MY STUDY BECAUSE YOU THREW A BRICK THROUGH MY WINDOW — WHAT DO YOU HAVE TO SAY FOR YOURSELF?
THERE ISN'T A WINDOW IN YOUR STUDY.
HEADMASTER
THERE IS.
ER... BUT IT ISN'T BROKEN.
HEAD MASTER
SEE FOR YOURSELF.
WELL, IT WASN'T ME
I HAVE WITNESSES WHO SAY YOU DID IT!
BUT IT WAS AN ACCIDENT!
HEADMASTER
YOUNG MAN, WHAT DO YOU WANT TO BE WHEN YOU GROW UP?
I WANT TO BE A BARRISTER!
HEADMASTER

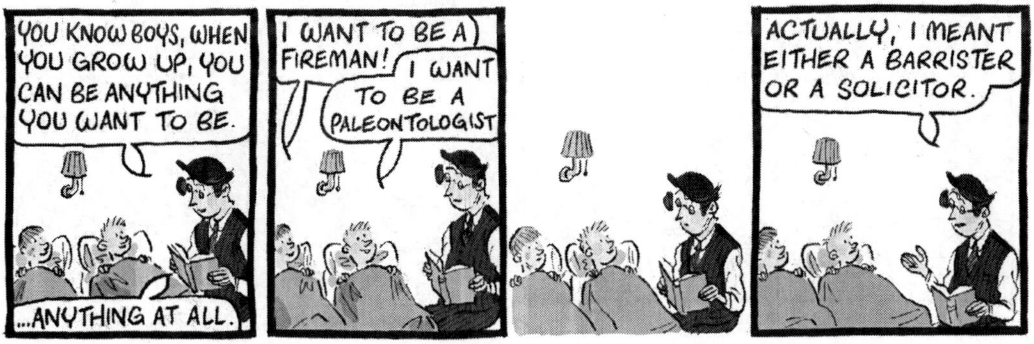

YOU KNOW BOYS, WHEN YOU GROW UP, YOU CAN BE ANYTHING YOU WANT TO BE.
...ANYTHING AT ALL.
I WANT TO BE A FIREMAN!
I WANT TO BE A PALEONTOLOGIST
ACTUALLY, I MEANT EITHER A BARRISTER OR A SOLICITOR.

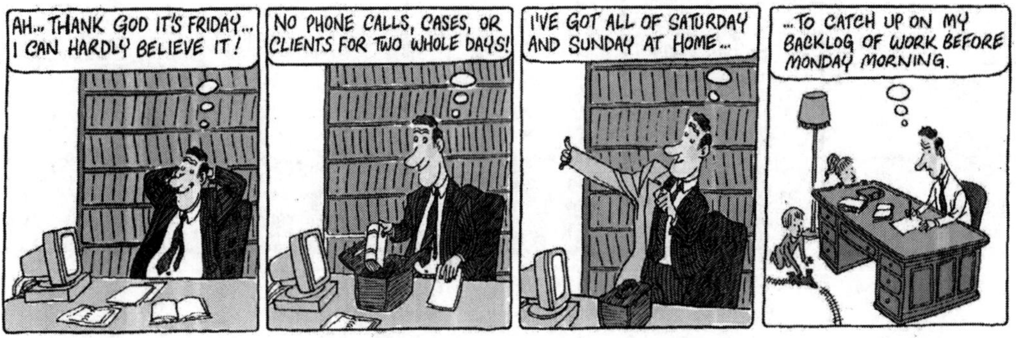

AH... THANK GOD IT'S FRIDAY... I CAN HARDLY BELIEVE IT!
NO PHONE CALLS, CASES, OR CLIENTS FOR TWO WHOLE DAYS!
I'VE GOT ALL OF SATURDAY AND SUNDAY AT HOME...
...TO CATCH UP ON MY BACKLOG OF WORK BEFORE MONDAY MORNING.

HM, LET'S SEE... CLAUSE 1(a) "ALL PARTIES SHALL ACT DILIGENTLY AND IN GOOD FAITH TO PERFORM THE TERMS HEREIN.
...ANY DISAGREEMENT IN LAW OR EQUITY SHALL BE DECIDED BY NEUTRAL BINDING ARBITRATION
THIS CONTRACT CONSTITUTES THE ENTIRE, FINAL AND EXCLUSIVE EXPRESSION OF THE AGREEMENT BETWEEN THE PARTIES.
OH DARLING – IT'S SO ROMANTIC DRAFTING OUR OWN PRE-NUPTIAL AGREEMENT TOGETHER.

GOLDILOCKS AND THE THREE BEARS!
AGAIN!? OH, ALL RIGHT... "ONCE UPON A TIME..."
A YOUNG GIRL OF INDETERMINATE AGE, LIVING WITHIN THE CURTILAGE OF A FOREST...
...PERAMBULATING TOWARDS THE DWELLING OF HER MATERNAL GRANDMOTHER, TRESPASSING VI ET ARMIS...
ZZZ

DADDY'S HAD A HARD WEEK SITTING AS A JUDGE, DARLING. TRY NOT TO PROVOKE HIM.
OK MUM.
DADDY... CAN I BORROW A TENNER?
HMF! WHAT DO YOU SAY?
PLEASE? PRETTY PLEASE?
PROD
BEST DADDY IN THE WHOLE WORLD?
HARUMPH!
YOUR HONOUR?
THAT'S BETTER.

JUST REMEMBER YOUR LINES, DARLING, AND THE TIPS I GAVE YOU, AND YOU'LL BE A BRILLIANT LADY MACBETH
YES DADDY
I HOPE YOU HAVEN'T MADE HER ALL NERVOUS, GEOFFREY.
NONSENSE, DEAR
I MERELY GAVE HER SOME IDEAS ON HOW TO MAKE THE PART MORE CONTEMPORARY.
IS THIS A DAGGER WHICH I SEE BEFORE ME, OR JUST A SHORT-BLADED TOOL DESIGNED FOR USE IN AND AROUND THE HOME?

LEAVING EARLY TODAY SIR GEOFFREY?
I'M OFF TO MY DAUGHTER'S CHRISTMAS PANTO. SHE'S PLAYING CINDARELLA YOU KNOW.
MY WICKED STEPMOTHER IS SO CRUEL, SHE MAKES ME WORK EIGHTY HOURS A WEEK, CLEANING AND SCRUBBING.
WHAT CAN I DO TO STOP HER FROM TREATING ME SO BADLY?
FILE A CLAIM FOR BREACH OF THE MAXIMUM WEEKLY HOURS PERMITTED UNDER THE WORKING TIME DIRECTIVE!

HARD DAY DEAR?
THE WORST, MOST EGREGIOUS CASE OF ADVERSE POSSESSION I HAVE EVER SEEN
WHAT'S THAT, DEAR?
"SQUATTER'S RIGHTS." THE CLAIMANT LACKS FORMAL TITLE, BUT OCCUPIES THE LAND ANYWAY.
I SEE, DEAR.
IT'S A SAD DAY WHEN A MAN CAN'T ENJOY HIS OWN PROPERTY IN PEACE.
...BUT WHY DON'T YOU JUST THROW THE DOG OFF THE SOFA IF YOU WANT TO SIT DOWN?
WHO DOES HE THINK RUNS THIS HOUSE ANYWAY?

WHAT DO YOU WANT?
TRICK OR TREAT!
WHAT DOES THAT MEAN?
ER... YOU GIVE US SWEETS, CHOCOLATES, THAT SORT OF THING.
WHAT- FOR FREE? DON'T I GET ANYTHING IN RETURN?
UM... NO...
IS IT TAX DEDUCTIBLE?
NO
AND PEOPLE ACTUALLY GIVE YOU THESE THINGS... FOR NOTHING?
UH-HUH
HM. WAIT HERE A MOMENT
TRICK OR TREAT!

GOT BAIL THEN, SIR GEOFFREY?
NO, I LOST AGAIN.
THESE APPLICATIONS ARE GETTING HARDER AND HARDER TO WIN... THEY KEEP CHANGING THE RULES!
SOMETIMES I FEAR THE LIBERTIES OF ENGLAND ARE AT AN END.
...BACK HOME TO THE WIFE, THEN?
I'M AFRAID SO. NO MORE LATE NIGHTS IN EL VINO'S

THERE IS NOT ONE SHRED OF FORENSIC EVIDENCE TO LINK THE ACCUSED TO THE MURDER WEAPON.
NOTHING YOU HAVE PRODUCED SO FAR WILL STAND UP IN COURT.
I SUGGEST YOU PULL YOURSELVES TOGETHER AND STOP TREATING THIS LIKE SOME SORT OF... OF...
GAME?
EXACTLY- COLONEL MUSTARD'S REPUTATION IS AT STAKE HERE.
YES, DADDY
CLUEDO

AS YOUR SOLICITOR I MUST ADVISE YOU OF THE TAX ADVANTAGES OF BEQUEATHING MONEY TO YOUR CHILDREN AS EARLY AS POSSIBLE.
SHAKE
IF YOU LEAVE THEM MOST OF YOUR ESTATE NOW, YOU REDUCE YOUR TAX BURDEN CONSIDERABLY.
I'VE PREPARED THE PAPERWORK, SO IF YOU'LL JUST SIGN HERE...
I WON'T SIGN A THING – YOU'RE NOT GETTING A PENNY UNTIL I'M DEAD!
NOW LOOK DAD, BE REASONABLE...

DADDY WAS IN COURT TODAY SO WE'RE ALL GOING TO WATCH HIM ON TELLY!
IT'S THE FIRST TIME THE PUBLIC HAVE SEEN ON TV WHAT GOES ON IN A COURT ROOM!
YOU'LL BE ABLE TO SEE ALL THE EXCITEMENT FOR YOURSELVES
M'LUD, I ASK FOR COSTS ON AN INDEMNITY BASIS PURSUANT TO SECTION 12 a OF THE
ZZZZZZ

CHAPTER TEN
LAWYERS ON HOLIDAY

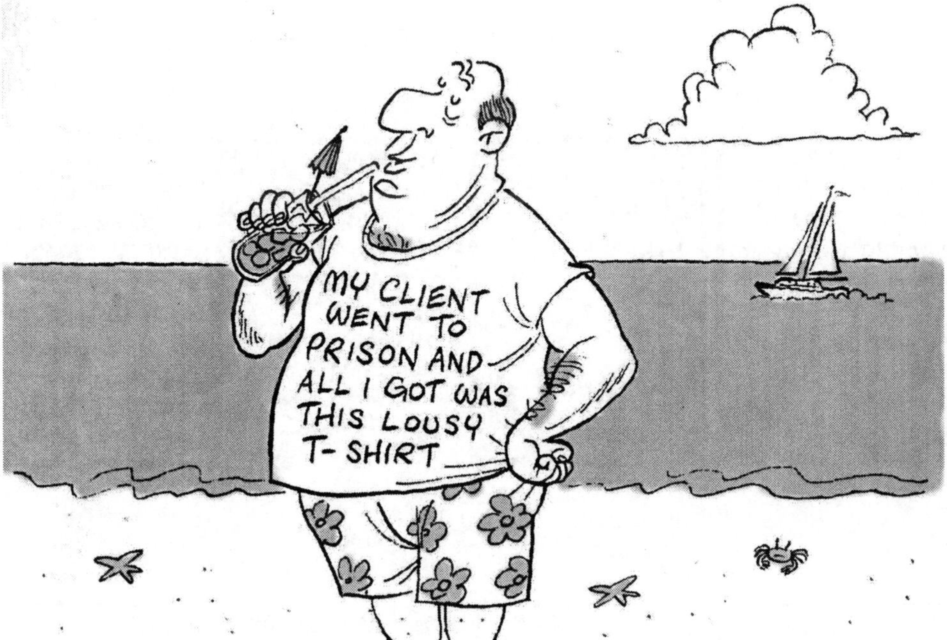
MY CLIENT WENT TO PRISON AND ALL I GOT WAS THIS LOUSY T-SHIRT

WHERE ARE YOU GOING ON HOLIDAY THIS YEAR? BACK TO TUSCANY?
YES, WITH EDWARD AND HIS FAMILY.
HM. YOU TWO GET ON WELL, CONSIDERING YOU WORK TOGETHER IN THE SAME DEPARTMENT.
OH... WE'VE BEEN GOING ON HOLIDAY TOGETHER FOR YEARS.
CLICK!
I COULDN'T IMAGINE GOING WITHOUT HIM NOW.
IT'S THE ONLY WAY I CAN STOP HIM STEALING MY CLIENTS WHILE I'M AWAY.

DARKEST CORNWALL AGAIN THIS YEAR? IS IT THE SANDY BEACHES THAT DRAW YOU BACK?
OH NO
THE CREAM TEAS?
NO
THE COASTAL PATH?
NO
RING!
AH, RACHEL, WE'LL NEED YOU TO BE IN TOUCH ON OUR CASE 24/7 THROUGH-OUT AUGUST...
OH DEAR, I'M AFRAID I'LL BE OUT OF REACH.
IT'S THE ONLY PLACE I KNOW OF WHERE MY BLACKBERRY DOESN'T WORK!
WHAT?!?

GOING ANYWHERE INTERESTING THIS YEAR, EDWARD?
TANZANIA I THINK. SAFARI WITH THE KIDS.
HELENA'S OFF TO INDONESIA FOR A FEW MONTHS.
NOTHING GLAMOROUS FOR ME – BORING OLD HOLLAND AGAIN THIS YEAR.
WHAT'S WITH ALL THE LONG HOLIDAYS?
NOT HOLIDAYS, CRAWLEY. HUMAN RIGHTS TRIBUNALS

WHERE DO LAWYERS GO ON HOLIDAY?
TAX LAWYER - CAYMAN ISLANDS
TAX CODE
FILM LAWYER - CANNES
CLICK!
FLASH!
CLICK!
INTERNATIONAL LITIGATOR - PARIS
ISTRO
VINS
TRAINEE SOLICITOR - NOWHERE

I CAN HARDLY BELIEVE IT! I'M ACTUALLY GETTING A HOLIDAY!
NO MORE OFFICE DRUDGERY FOR A WHOLE WEEK!
I CAN RELAX, ENJOY MYSELF...
BAR
GET MYSELF A BIG DRINK...
AND GET SOME WORK DONE WITHOUT ANY INTERRUPTIONS
SEE YOU AT DINNERTIME

HERE'S YOUR £1 MILLION BRIEF FEE, SIR GEOFFREY.
LOVELY.
WELL, I'M OFF TO BARBADOS.
BUT WE'RE PAYING YOU £1 MILLION TO WORK ON OUR CASE!
OH... DON'T WORRY, I'LL TAKE IT WITH ME.
Z Z Z

WHAT DO LAWYERS DO AT THE BEACH?
① TAX LAWYER
FINANCE ACT
② CRIMINAL LAWYER
INSPECTOR MORSE
③ BARRISTER
RUMPOLE OF THE BAILEY
④ LITIGATION LAWYER
OK, PHONE THE COURT AND TRY TO GET US A POSTPONEMENT...
...AND FAX THE OTHER SIDE'S SOLICITORS.
...AND TELL THE CLIENT I'LL BE IN THE FIRST PLANE BACK
tele

HOLIDAY LATIN for Lawyers
Bona Vacantia
Forum Conveniens
CLICK!
Subpoena Colada
SLURP!
Habeas Corpus

HELLO SIR GEOFFREY, HOW IS YOUR FACT-FINDING MISSION TO GUANTANAMO GOING?
IT'S PURE HELL HERE, DEREK.
...THE HEAT, THE OVERCROWDED CONDITIONS...
THESE PEOPLE ARE BEING DENIED THEIR BASIC HUMAN RIGHTS!
WHERE ARE YOU? IN THE DETAINEE HOLDING AREA?
NO. HEATHROW AIRPORT.

OH DEAR... I WONDER IF I FILED THOSE PLEADINGS BEFORE THE LIMITATION PERIOD EXPIRED ?
DID I MISS ANY OF THE AUTHORITIES IN THE CORPORATE DEBENTURE LITIGATION ?
DID I GET BACK TO EVERYONE ON MY CALL LIST BEFORE I LEFT?
WAS COUNSEL PROPERLY INSTRUCTED ?
YOU'RE BACK FROM HOLIDAY EARLY, RACHEL. SOMETHING WRONG ?
WAY TOO MUCH STRESS

THIS IS THE LIFE! NO MORE LAW FOR WEEKS! ALL MY PAPERS FILED...
WITNESSES PROOFED, COUNSEL BRIEFED...
EXPERTS INSTRUCTED, NOTHING FORGOTTEN.
DID YOU REMEMBER TO FILE THE CLAIM BEFORE THE LIMITATION PERIOD EXPIRED?

IT'S URGENT– I MUST SPEAK TO MR LOOPHOLE
I'M AFRAID HE'S ON HOLIDAY.
WELL, DIDN'T HE LEAVE ANY INSTRUCTIONS IN THE FILE?
I DON'T KNOW, I'M JUST A TEMP...
ER... HOLD ON, THERE DOES SEEM TO BE A NOTE HERE.
IT SAYS "THIS CLIENT IS A COMPLETE FUSSPOT. FOB HIM OFF WITH SOME STORY AND I'LL DEAL WITH HIM WHEN I GET BACK."
HELLO?
CLICK!
IT'S SO NICE TO GO AWAY KNOWING THAT EVERYTHING HAS BEEN TAKEN CARE OF AT THE OFFICE.

WELCOME BACK FROM HOLIDAY, RACHEL. THERE'S A STACK OF PHONE MESSAGES FOR YOU.
YOU HAVE: 3,053 unopened emails...
TAP TAP
... AND HERE ARE YOUR FILES THAT ARE NOW EXTREMELY URGENT.
...OH, AND WHILE YOU WERE AWAY WE MOVED TWO NEW TRAINEES INTO YOUR OFFICE.
HI!
MEET ANDY AND VANESSA
I'M NEVER GOING ON HOLIDAY AGAIN.
SO... ARE YOU GLAD TO BE BACK?

SO HOW WERE YOUR HOLIDAYS, SIR GEOFFREY?
OH... LOTS OF QUALITY TIME WITH THE CHILDREN.
...NO WORK TO TAKE ME AWAY FROM FAMILY LIFE.
PLENTY OF BOARD GAMES, CARDS AND DAY TRIPS.
SAD TO BE BACK THEN?
GOOD GOD NO. I COULDN'T HAVE PUT UP WITH IT ANOTHER DAY.

THAT'S AGREED THEN. OUR RESPECTIVE CLIENTS WILL TAKE THIS DISPUTE TO ARBITRATION.
GENEVA? YES, THAT'S FINE. BIT OF A TREK, OF COURSE.
WELL... WE MUSTN'T GRUMBLE. ALL IN THE LINE OF DUTY, EH?
ANY SKI PLANS THIS WINTER, RICHARD?
...JUST BOOKED A HOLIDAY TO SWITZERLAND.
SOUNDS EXPENSIVE
...FUNNILY ENOUGH, NOT AT ALL.

I KNOW YOU'VE BEEN WORKING CRAZY HOURS ON THIS TAKEOVER, CRAWLEY...
...BUT WE'VE GOT TO PULL ALL THE STOPS.
OK, RICHARD.
NOSES TO THE GRINDSTONE, BACKS TO THE WHEEL, EH?
OF COURSE, RICHARD.
I'M ALWAYS AT THE END OF THE PHONE IF YOU NEED ME.
THANKS, RICHARD.
... AND REMEMBER CRAWLEY... IT'S ALL DOWNHILL FROM HERE.

AREN'T YOU GLAD I DRAGGED YOU AWAY FROM THE LAW FOR A WEEK, DARLING?
ISN'T IT BREATHTAKING?
EXTRAORDINARY!
STAGGERING!
I'M LOST FOR WORDS... I'VE NEVER SEEN ANYTHING LIKE IT!
I MEAN — THIS CLAUSE IS CLEARLY UNREASONABLE!
THERE'S NO WAY THAT WOULD GET PAST THE UNFAIR CONTRACT TERMS ACT!
SKI HIRE TERMS & CONDITIONS

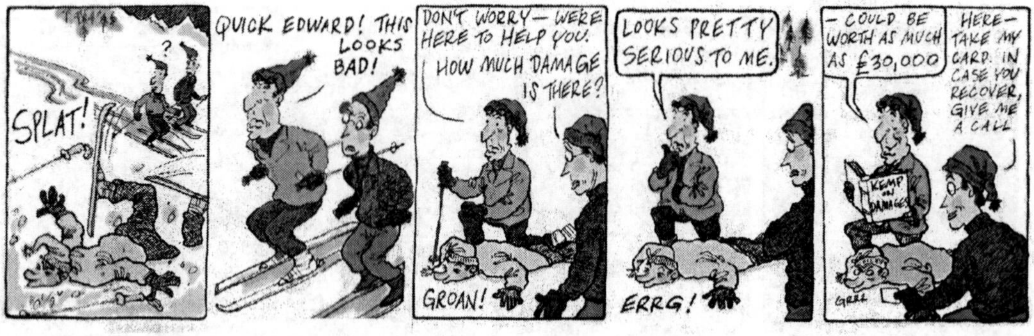
SPLAT!
QUICK EDWARD! THIS LOOKS BAD!
DON'T WORRY— WE'RE HERE TO HELP YOU.
HOW MUCH DAMAGE IS THERE?
GROAN!
LOOKS PRETTY SERIOUS TO ME.
ERRG!
— COULD BE WORTH AS MUCH AS £30,000
HERE— TAKE MY CARD. IN CASE YOU RECOVER, GIVE ME A CALL
KEMP ON DAMAGES

CHAPTER ELEVEN
LIFE BEYOND LAW

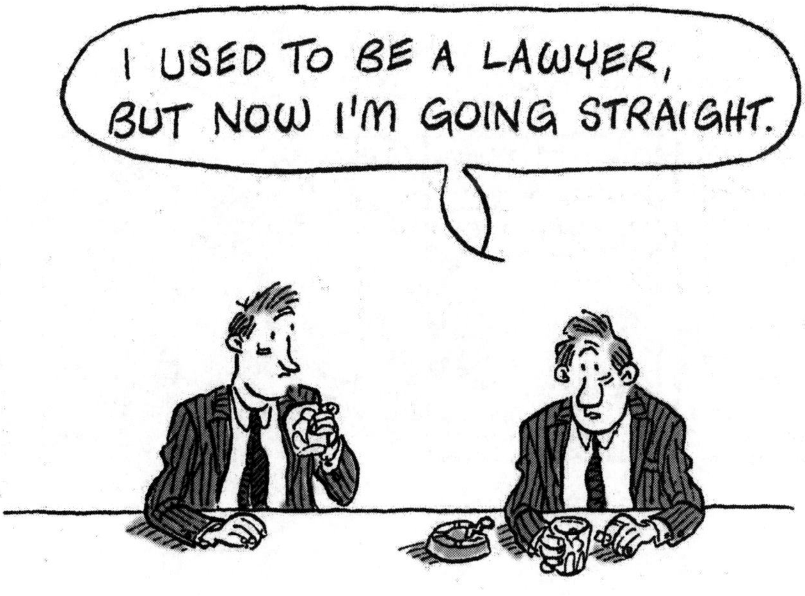
I USED TO BE A LAWYER,
BUT NOW I'M GOING STRAIGHT.

ARE YOU COMING TO THE PARTY ON FRIDAY?
WHAT PARTY?
OH...IT'S A STAYING DO FOR A FEW OF THE TEAM
WHAT'S A STAYING DO?
WELL, SO MANY PEOPLE ARE LEAVING THE FIRM, WE'VE GIVEN UP HAVING LEAVING DO'S.
SO WE THOUGHT WE'D HAVE A STAYING DO FOR THE ONES WHO ARE STILL HERE.

RICHARD, I'VE HAD IT! IF YOU DON'T REDUCE MY WORKLOAD, I'M GOING TO QUIT!
JUST DRAFT THIS STATEMENT WOULD YOU?
I MEAN IT! IF THINGS DON'T IMPROVE, I'M LEAVING!
UM...OK
JUST SKIM THE CASE AUTHORITY FIRST.
I REALLY MEAN IT YOU KNOW!
SLAM!
I HEAR RACHEL QUIT. OVERWORK, APPARENTLY.
REALLY? WHY DIDN'T SHE TELL ANYONE SHE WAS UNHAPPY?

I'M SO SORRY TO HEAR ABOUT YOUR NEPHEW'S CAR ACCIDENT, SIR GEOFFREY.
IT'S BEEN GHASTLY.
HE'S SUFFERED SOME...MENTAL DAMAGE...
I HAD WANTED HIM TO GO TO THE BAR, BUT NOW WE MAY HAVE TO PUT HIM IN AN INSTITUTION!
SURELY YOU DON'T MEAN...?
YES. THE ONLY THING LEFT FOR HIM NOW IS...
...INVESTMENT BANKING!
HOW HORRIBLE!

I LOVE BEING A LAWYER. WELL, APART FROM THE LONG HOURS OF COURSE.
AND THE ENDLESS AGGRAVATION.
... AND THE BORING DOCUMENTS, AND THE REPETITIVE WORK.
... THE HOSTILE COLLEAGUES, THE GRUMPY CLIENTS...
SO WHAT IS THE BIT YOU LOVE, EXACTLY?
I CAN'T REMEMBER.

...SO IN THE END THE WHOLE CASE TURNED ON THE PROMISSORY ESTOPPEL ARGUMENT.
VERY INTERESTING EDWARD.
...BUT I THINK THAT IS QUITE ENOUGH LAW DON'T YOU?
LET'S DISCUSS SOMETHING ELSE FOR A CHANGE.
... ANYONE SEEN THE NEW GUIDELINES ON THE CALCULATION OF LOST EARNINGS IN PERSONAL INJURY CLAIMS?
YES INDEED
FASCINATING.

I HATE MY JOB, I HATE THE LAW, I HATE THIS FIRM.
I HAVE TO GET AWAY FROM ALL THIS.
THAT'S IT... I'M GOING TO QUIT... I'LL DO IT NOW!
KNOCK! KNOCK!
SORRY RACHEL, BUT THE FIRM IS DOWNSIZING, AND WE'RE GOING TO HAVE TO LET YOU GO.
NOOOO!!!
I WANT TO STAY!

SORRY RACHEL... DOWN-TURN IN THE MARKET... THERE'S NO ROOM FOR YOU HERE RIGHT NOW.
NO HARD FEELINGS.
WELCOME TO MEGA PLC, RICHARD. WE'RE LOOKING FORWARD TO YOUR FIRM'S PRESENT-ATION.
MEGA PL
OUR NEW IN-HOUSE SOLICITOR, RACHEL, WILL EVALUATE YOUR PERFORMANCE.
HELLO RICHARD.
ER... HELLO RACHEL.
SORRY RICHARD, DOWN-TURN IN THE MARKET... THERE'S NO ROOM FOR YOU HERE RIGHT NOW.
MEGA PLC
...NO HARD FEELINGS.

TIMES ARE TOUGH. WE HAVE TO LOSE SOME STAFF. WHO WILL IT BE... HIGGS?
HE'S USELESS... BUT HIS UNCLE IS IN THE HOUSE OF LORDS.
OH. WELL...
...HOW ABOUT PHILIPS?
HMM... NO... HE ORGANIZES GOLF WEEKENDS FOR CLIENTS.
... AND HE MIXES A MEAN MARTINI.
ELLIS?
SHE'S A BRILLIANT LAWYER... TOTAL WORKAHOLIC. BILLS FOUR TIMES HER SALARY.
YEAH... SHE MAKES THE REST OF US LOOK BAD.
OK. ELLIS IT IS THEN.

DOWNSHIFTING -HOW IT WORKS:
① QUIT YOUR HIGHLY PAID JOB WITH INSANE HOURS.
YOU'RE LEAVING THE FIRM?
YES... TO GET MY LIFE BACK!
② FIND A PART-TIME JOB.
WE CAN'T PAY YOU MUCH, BUT YOU CAN WORK A FOUR DAY WEEK!
I'LL TAKE IT!
③ PART-TIME BECOMES FULL-TIME.
ER... WE'RE A BIT SHORT-STAFFED... CAN YOU WORK LATE TONIGHT?
UM... OK...
④ WELCOME TO YOUR NEW LOW-PAID JOB WITH INSANE HOURS.
SIGH!

I'M FED UP WITH THE BAR. THE PUBLIC THINK WE'RE ALL FAT CATS, BUT LEGAL AID HARDLY PAYS ANY-THING THESE DAYS.
I'VE GOT TO GET OUT, DO SOMETHING ELSE.
LIKE WHAT?
THAT'S THE TROUBLE! WHAT ELSE AM I QUALIFIED TO DO THAT PAYS A DECENT LIVING?
HELLO... 4 LAWN BUILDINGS. I'LL PUT YOU THROUGH TO SIR GEOFFREY NOW...
CLERK'S ROOM

WE STRONGLY FAVOUR PRO BONO WORK HERE AT THE FIRM.
ACTUALLY, WE TOLERATE IT.
WE HAVE SEVERAL CLIENTS WE ACT FOR ON A PRO BONO BASIS
THEY REFUSE TO PAY OUR HUGE BILLS.
WE ENCOURAGE ALL OUR ASSOCIATES TO DO PRO BONO WORK.
ONCE THEY'VE LEFT THE FIRM.
IN FACT, WE HAVE A PRIZE FOR THE LAWYER WHO DOES THE MOST.
IT'S CALLED A P45.

YOU KNOW, I OFTEN WONDER IF THERE ISN'T SOMETHING ELSE WE COULD DO, OTHER THAN PRACTICE LAW.
SUCH AS?
THAT'S THE TROUBLE... I DON'T KNOW WHAT ELSE TO DO.
WELL... YOU COULD DO ANYTHING!
LIKE WHAT?
ANYTHING! WE ARE ONLY LIMITED BY THE SCOPE OF OUR IMAG-INATIONS!
SIGH! BACK TO WORK THEN.

The Queen's Counsel Official Lawyer's Handbook
DANIEL R. WHITE AND ALEX WILLIAMS

The Queen's Counsel Official Lawyer's Handbook

The Queen's Counsel is a cartoon satire on law and lawyers appearing on Thursdays in the law pages of The Times. Collecting together the very best of the cartoon strip with the sagest of lawyerly advice The Queen's Counsel Official Lawyer's Handbook is the ultimate guide to surviving a legal career.

Tips include: *How to get into a top law firm and stay there, racking up billable hours the easy way , Partnership you can make it – if you know what to kiss, and whose Understanding what lawyers do and how to stop them doing it to you.*

available at www.qccartoon.com

Lightning Source UK Ltd.
Milton Keynes UK
UKOW02f2214261113

221911UK00008B/86/P